On Beginning from Within

By

DOUGLAS V. STEERE

Haverford College

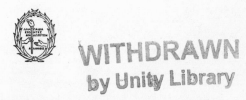

New York and London

HARPER & BROTHERS PUBLISHERS

ON BEGINNING FROM WITHIN

TO

D., H., AND A.

THE BEST OF COMPANIONS

CONTENTS

CONTENTS

PREFACE

THESE essays are concerned with the intensification of the life of God in the individual hearts of men. They examine successively the relation of the saint to society, the source of the authority that a saint exercises among his fellows, the nurture of the inward life by a new set of devotional exercises, the debt of theology to devotion, and the prospect of death as an agency of individuation and as a power for awakening man to his dependence upon God.

The final essay was given at Harvard University on April 14, 1942, as the Ingersoll Lecture. The first four essays were given at Harvard University in March and April, 1943, as the William Belden Noble Lectures. Parts of them were previously delivered at the Episcopal Theological Seminary in Virginia on the Reinicker Foundation, and at the Chicago Theological Seminary on the Alden Tuthill Lecture Foundation. For the encouragement of these occasions and for gracious hospitality I am indebted to Dean Willard Sperry, Dean Wallace Rollins, and President Albert Palmer.

DOUGLAS V. STEERE

Haverford, Pa.
June 30, 1943

ON BEGINNING FROM WITHIN

CHAPTER I

THE SAINT AND SOCIETY

~~~~~~

IN LIBERAL Protestant Christian circles today we are consumed with a passion for a new design for society. We
are told that if we had only had a more inclusive League
of Nations, or a broad federal union of the democratic
states, or a world economic league, or a world government,
this last and any future wars could have been, or could in
the future be eliminated, and that men could live undis-
turbed in a peaceful brotherhood together.

The social revolutionaries within and without the
church do not let us off so easily; but they, too, claim that
if the workers of the world could use their respective states
to advance the interests of a classless society, men could
really achieve a life of peaceful brotherhood, and that
prosperity for all is within reach. The social conservatives
claim that, given another chance, they could, by a stream-
lined program of managerial control, effect a remarkable
prosperity for the brotherhood of man and leave to us
most of our civil liberties in the bargain. Brotherhood
and prosperity are spread out on many counters today,
and unusual bargains in brotherhood are being pressed
upon us.

But as the weary struggle of our time grinds on,
who is there among us who has not by day or by

night begun to hear voices, voices that query the price at which this merchandise is offered to us, or at which we offer it to others? That structural changes must come in society is not in question. But to these vast horizontal solutions that are now being discussed, solutions that would redeem by extending what has already broken down, or by multiplying the same elements, or by transposing the same unstable fractions, the voice within us keeps repeating quietly but resolutely, "Bargains in brotherhood, occupational therapy, busy work." And a curious vision appears in which one group of harried and frantic lunatics are at work ripping strips of cloth apart, and another group of very sober and depressed lunatics are at work sewing the strips back together again, but into ever larger quilts. The voice continues, monotonously, "Busy work, occupational therapy, bargains in brotherhood."

An Eastern sociologist has expressed this idea formally in discussing the ripeness of our time for the emergence of a new religion or the regeneration of an older religion.

The respective societies were preserved from dissolution not so much through the "practical and expert" manipulation of economic, political, genetic or other factors, but mainly through the transmutation of values, the spiritualization of conduct and the ennoblement of social relations effected through the medium of religion.[1]

A friend of mine sent to Dr. Egbert Munzer, of St. Xavier University in Nova Scotia, a copy of an excellent plan which he had devised for merging some of the public utilities of the European states in the post-war

[1] Sorokin, *The Crisis of Our Age*, pp. 322f.

period, and after a careful criticism of its details, Dr. Munzer wrote:

The future will not belong to the organizers or the politicians of the traditional type, but to the saints and the prophets, and thus to the religionists, and it will be *they* who become the creators, neither capitalism nor socialism which after all are fundamentally the same, inverted and twisted but intrinsically related *querelles domestiques*.

WHAT HAS A SAINT TO DO WITH ORDER?

To modern Protestant Christian ears there is something shocking about such a statement. What after all could a saint do to stop a war? What could a saint do after a war is over to heal society's terrible weariness and want? What has a saint to do with *order*? What has a saint to do with such forms of order as politics or economics, anyway? Did not the saint make his exit from serious social influence when world organization supplanted the individual witness? Is not a saint an extreme form of the Christian as an "individual" and is the saint, therefore, not at one pole and society at the other? What beyond a rhetorical statement can be meant by calling the saints creators of society and prophesying that the future of society is in their hands?

On the evening of December 11, 1941, the date of Germany's declaration of war against the United States, a distinguished German guest of Haverford College delivered a brilliant lecture. He maintained that the spiritual roots of the Christian religion had furnished the tradition in which an indigenous democracy in Switzerland, along the German Rhine, and especially in the old Hanseatic cities of the north of Germany, had developed even earlier than in England. He went on to show the stubborn persistence of this spirit up to the eighteenth century and beyond. He admitted, however, that the acids of seventeenth-century science, the attacks of eighteenth-century rationalism, the Marxian anti-religious influence on the workers in the nineteenth century, and the general secularism of the twentieth century had eaten away much of that religious stem, and that the yielding of these long-held rights of local privilege in the present chaotic century was a culmination of this. He insisted that only a spiritual revival in Germany could restore the ground for a lasting democracy by renewing this religious stem.

I visited him some months later and pressed him to indicate precisely in what form such a spiritual revival in Germany might come about. It could only come, he insisted, by the appearance of a saint, one who felt in his own body and mind all the suffering and agony through which his people were going, and yet who transcended it. By his life and the life of a band of lay followers who might appear as some new and free order, "men and women very holy but who did not fear to die," the people could alone be raised to a higher level of generous devotion to God and their fellows.

He sketched a picture of lost opportunity in what happened after 1918 in the Roman Catholic church. This church and the Social Democratic party were almost the only institutions in Germany to emerge from that war without being discredited. The Church had a magnificent opportunity. What did the Church do with it in this revolutionary situation where for five years the people in their molten condition could have been won for the highest life? Instead of a saint and perhaps a new religious order, as has happened so many times before in the revolutionary crises of history, the Church seemed infertile and bore no such child. Instead, she went in for horizontal expansion, a vast increase of property—churches, schools, seminaries, a political party—and the spiritual life of the country continued its decline. If there is again no saint, no band of spiritually devoted laity to rouse the longing life of the spirit in the German people, there can be no lasting political integrity that will spawn institutions that respect the individual as a sacred being.

SOCIETY'S VULNERABLE CENTER

This unusual analysis does not overlook the vast complexity of forces that are at work upon society. Yet, it seems to turn society over and find at the back of it, as Plato contended, "a man writ large." There, behind society's outer façade of toughness, this analysis maintains that there is, and must always be, a center that is peculiarly vulnerable to the life of a man or to a band of men who might exemplify society's deepest yearning and call out a response from it that would alone make any enduring structural changes possible.

It is not easy to describe this vulnerable center of society where it is open to change by the saint, by the Christian individual. Rousseau's "general will" was a mystical approach to its political significance. The sense of decency and fair play and equity that is never more than very partially embodied in law but that can sooner or later overthrow law if law violates it; the center in society to which the much-discussed group ethos or *consensus gentium* refers—these are arrows pointing in its direction. Their testimony would seem to bear out the observation that at the vulnerable center in society there is a dream, a vision, a purpose, and that dream, that purpose, is continually in the process of slipping out of focus or of being sharply refocused again as society lunges on its titanic course.

There is a good deal of reason to believe that this center is as intimately connected with the corporate institutions of society as the nerve center of inner consent is connected with the habit mechanisms of an individual person. At that point we are often aware of how much a habit system depends upon this center of consent to continue. I remember as a young teacher in lecturing to my classes at Haverford College how I fell into a fairly common unconscious device for ransoming time in order to think of what I was to say next, by saying, ". . . so to speak." A student-friend pointed out to me that the boys were laying wagers on how many of these rest-period so-to-speak's would appear in a class hour, and that more attention was being paid to these tabulations than to what I said. I thanked him and resolved then and there that there would be no more so-to-speak's, for they were quite effectively thwarting my deeper desire to be a good teacher. The habit mechanism was well established, however, and although consent had been vehemently withdrawn, I found myself in the middle of a lecture the next day with "so to" already out, and "speak" well on the way. I stopped short, forgot what I was trying to say, went through what seemed a long period of complete amnesia, then things began to function again, and I went on. I do not believe that I have ever used that phrase since that morning unless it was consciously chosen. When the center of consent is withdrawn by the incongruity of the habit and the dream, the habit mechanism itself is in jeopardy.

In England fifteen years ago I knew a highly-trained naval engineer, of about thirty-nine or forty, married and with a family to support. He was engaged in designing torpedoes at the Naval Engineering laboratories at Teddington. In the course of the years that followed the last war, he had become a believer in the complete futility of war to accomplish its aims and in total disarmament. Yet, with consent gone, each day he set out for his torpedo-designing and testing laboratory, because the training and habit mechanisms of his life and his family responsibilities still held him in their grip. I was not surprised three or four years later to find him in this country, having made the break, and now in middle life in a research position in a large professional school. When consent gives way and the nerve of even the stoutest habit patterns dies, the collapse of those patterns or their replacement by others is not likely to be far off, although in the interval, to a superficial observer, the façade of the habit mechanisms may seem quite as substantial as ever. When Augustine experienced his striking conversion to Christ in a garden of Milan, at the age of thirty-two, he was engaged in lecturing as Professor of Rhetoric. The nerve of this professional life was clipped at that point, and he knew he must change it. But his *Confessions* tell us that he continued to lecture as usual until the harvest time when the semester ended. During that time an outside observer might have noted little change. And yet he had already abandoned completely what looked so stable and so fixed.

It is at this fluid center of the dream, the purpose, the inner yearning of both an individual and of society that habit systems and corporate institutions have to be continually confirmed if they are to live, and a wise predictor of the future course of any individual or of any society will be as much or more concerned with detecting the state of this center as with any study of individual habits or of social institutions. It is only the superficial critic who is taken in by the apparent staunchness, the too, too solid flesh of the façade. The façade-error is a striking example of "the fallacy of misplaced concretion."

Carl Sandburg in his *The People, Yes,* has written of the deceitful appearance of the husks of power:

> The czar has eight million men with guns and bayonets.
> Nothing can happen to the czar.
> The czar is the voice of God and shall live forever.
> Turn and look at the forest of steel and cannon
> Where the czar is guarded by eight million soldiers.
> Nothing can happen to the czar!
> They said that for years and in the summer of 1914
> In the Year of Our Lord Nineteen Hundred and Fourteen
> As a portent and an assurance they said with owl faces:
> "Nothing can happen to the czar."
> Yet the czar and his bodyguard of eight million vanished.

Back of the hard façade, at the fluid, vulnerable center where the dream, the purpose, the core of consent of any society is to be found, one always finds a man, and a man's wants, and before it is plumbed a man's deepest wants. That is why Irving Babbit can write so plausibly in the opening page of his *Democracy and Leadership* that "when studied with any degree of thoroughness, the economic problem will be found to run into the political problem, the political problem in turn into the philosophical problem, and the philosophical problem itself to be almost indissolubly bound up at last with the religious problem."

In other words, what does man most deeply want? And are the habit mechanisms of his personal life or of the social institutions of his time at diametrical cross-purposes with what he wants; or are they roughly headed in the same direction?

Alfred Noyes in his analysis of the dilemma of our time is doing more than to present *The New York Times'* monotonous Monday morning summaries of clergymen's conclusions "that the world is in a bad way because it has forgotten God," when, in his *The Edge of the Abyss*, he writes:

> We must look deeper than the political and economic catastrophes of the modern world if we would find the real cause of the contemporary tragedy. The cause of the tragedy is neither political nor economic. It is that the race has been induced to forget its true end through which happiness (Carlyle's blessedness) alone can come.

THE NATURE OF THE SAINT

Now the Christian saint (and the saint is a Christian individual in full degree and nothing more) is not in the first instance concerned with society or society's redemption. He is not a device for reaching and improving society as such. Yet, he does precisely that. The saint is rather a man or a woman who has become clear as to exactly what he wants of all there is in the world, and whom a love at the heart of things has so satisfied that he gaily reduces his cargo to make for that port. "Oh God, my Lord, do as thou wilt; I will be still." He is one who is doing what he wants to do, not what he wants to do this minute, and the next minute, and the next minute, but what beneath the minutes and the days and the years he would want to do if all of them should vanish and leave him forever at it. He is responding, answering back to the love of God in whatever setting he may be placed. He is a radical in the true sense of that word, for he has gone to the root of things and found the root good. He is holy in the sense of the totality of his abandonment to that Loving One.

Leon Bloy's hunger for this goal expressed itself in a single classic line, "There is only one sorrow, not to be a saint." From the inside out, the saint's life is the life of joy.

Beloved in thine own heart the holy tree is growing there,
From joy the holy branches start, and all the trembling flowers
they bear.

It is the only kind of life that deeply satisfies, and it is only those who write from the outside in, that can picture what these saints did as one of sheer sacrifice.

This joy, however, does not come of the saint himself. It seems to come from what the saint has found. And his fellows find in him or through him what he has found. As Jacopone da Todi puts it, a saint is "one in whom Christ is felt to live again." And on this earth this is the greatest miracle of all—for Christ to be felt to live again.

Among unsophisticated people this is the way truth is always detected. Dr. Van Ess, the great Christian missionary to Iraq, once told me of a missionary's sermon in Iraq to a group of simple Arabs on what Jesus was like. One brightened up and said, "I have met him." The missionary frowned and explained once again that he lived nineteen hundred years ago, and so he could not possibly have met him. "No," the native insisted, "I have met him." And it turned out that a Swedish doctor who lived and healed and worked among a tribe some distance away so fitted the missionary's description of Jesus as to rouse that quiver of recognition in the Arab.

Dr. Rambo told of saying good-bye to an old Indian woman on the steps of his dispensary in mid-India, after having successfully operated on her eyes for cataracts. Now as she went away, seeing, she bowed low and said, "Good-bye, God." Dr. Rambo hastily explained that he was not God, but only a poor weak servant of His. But she would have none of it, and as she went on down the road she turned every little way and waved gratefully shouting, "Good-bye, God, good-bye, God." A saint is one in whom God or Christ is felt to live again.

These men and women in whom their fellows feel the miracle of Christ's return have about them a number of qualities which it would be well to focus upon before returning directly to their influence upon this vulnerable center in society where the dream is hid.

THE SAINT AND THE PERSONAL REVOLUTION

In the first place, the saint is one who begins with himself and with what he must do, not with denunciations of society and its wrongs. He is a witness to the personal revolution although he seldom stops there. He approves of the sentiments of the old negro spiritual that chants, " 'Tain't the preacher nor the deacon but 'tis me, Oh Lord, a-standin' in the need of prayer." And he would well understand Unamuno's remark that the way to get rid of lying is to get rid of one liar, although he would be confident that he could never do this in his own strength alone. At this point the saint is to be sharply distinguished from many social, revolutionary leaders who see no connection whatever between their own personal lives and conduct and the "cause" to which they dedicate themselves with such abandon and who have faith that if you change the outer situation, personal change will occur of itself. As the saint finds his life laid open before the scrutiny of the All-Loving One, he is acutely aware that all of the projected sins of society are present within himself. And with God's help he is concerned to begin from within, in Maritain's words, "to purify the springs of history within his own heart." Catherine of Siena, some of whose later political and social concerns we shall have occasion to note, started where she was and with herself. She began her life of abandon to God in years of the most exacting household drudgery for her demanding family by day, in prayer by night. Francis of Assisi began a task of building under sealed orders from within and spent years at it before he had either disciples or a message.

Having begun with the first person singular, there is no naïveté about the world's natural goodness among the saints. Nor is there any of the social revolutionary's naïveté about the automatic character of making all men good by the manipulation of the political or economic environment. The saint knows sin for what it is because he knows it within himself. Yet, the saint is not overcome by sin, for he knows the Light by which the darkness is revealed as darkness; and his trust is in that Light.

There is a profound principle of order revealed in the point at which the saint begins the Christian revolution. Pascal defined order as "consisting principally in digressions upon each point to relate it to the end and to keep the end always in sight." For the saint to begin relating society to the end, when the end was not in sight for his own life, would be absurd. Hence he begins with the relation of his own life to the end, and with the end deeply aroused within himself, he goes on to relate all that he touches to the true end, keeping the end always in sight.

This principle of order makes each detail of the saint's life no longer a detail or a digression when it has been related to the end. And his scrupulous care over what to the world may seem a trifle can only be understood in terms of this rigorous inner logic of order. E. Herman has expressed this with striking simplicity in her *Creative Prayer*:

When we read the lives of the saints, we are struck by a certain large leisure which went hand in hand with a remarkable effectiveness. They were never hurried. They did comparatively few things, and these not necessarily striking or important; and they troubled very little about their influence. Yet, they always seemed to hit the mark; every bit of their life *told*. Their simplest actions had a distinction, an exquisiteness which suggested the artist. The reason is not far to seek. Their sainthood lay in their habit of referring the smallest actions to God. They lived in God. They acted from a pure motive of love towards God. They were as free from self-regard as from slavery to the good opinion of others. God's Son and God rewarded; what else needed they? Hence the inalienable dignity of these meek, quiet figures that seem to produce such marvelous effects with such humble materials.[2]

Because of the saint's pains with his bearings, he may have significance for society beyond all other men as a bench mark to which society may return in revolutionary periods in order to resurvey her course.

[2] P. 28.

THE JOYOUS HEROISM OF THE SAINT

In the second place, there is in the true Christian saint a simple unassuming heroism that stops at nothing when his witness to his dearest love is at stake. For Christian saints are sons of One who made the cross a symbol of victory. St. Lawrence as he lay dying refused the offer of a mattress, saying, "My Saviour died not on a feather-bed but on the hard wood of the cross," and this temper, to take what comes without softening it for themselves, marks these men and women throughout Christian history. Telemachus quite deliberately threw away his life, a fool for Christ's sake, instead of saving it in order to write pamphlets or sermons against the iniquities of the arena. By his act he finally abolished the gladiatorial contests in Rome. Francis Xavier left Spain as a young man knowing in his heart that he would never return, in order to carry the message of Christ to India and the Far East. A little Quaker band set out from Rhode Island for Boston where their form of worship was forbidden under pain of death. The women in the company carried with them the linen in which to wrap the bodies of those of their number who would be hanged. Father Damien served the lepers on Molochai with his own body. "There was not a pot or pan on Molochai that Damien had not washed." Finally he died a leper's death himself.

These are only dramatic reminders of the inward power of the Christian saints to stop at nothing. Whether we note these dramatic reminders or recall the hidden ones where in the household, the office, on the farm, on beds of pain, this same heroic power is felt, these men and women reveal the nature of the Christian commitment by having torn up any return-trip ticket, by having cut off forever their road back to an easy middle course of life. You can't go home again. To regard them is to suffer a frontal attack upon the safety factor with which most of us seek to surround our lives.

A short time ago I had a letter from a boy who is a conscientious objector to war and with whom I had worked when I visited a Civilian Public Service Camp in North Carolina. He had been there for over a year working at hard manual labor. He wrote, "Somewhere among us are the roots of our real concerns. In the summer volunteer camps life was ideal and hardly in earnest. There was a road back for every man who didn't go forward. There was money to spend and a short, happy summer to think wonderfully-vital thoughts in. I'm convinced that this is a stronger brew in the Civilian Public Service Camps. There isn't a road back and there isn't financial security. The time is heavy and long, and the project is important only as we are internally vital. This is a stiffer proposition, and I think we are getting a great deal out of it." No, for the saint, there is no road back, only forward, and forward it is, over a path that calls for the sandals of faith.

Franz Werfel has pictured this "all or none" decision with unusual discernment in his recent *Song of Bernadette* where the Dean is asking Bernadette severely whether she knows what her persistence in this way may cost her.

Dean Peyramale was silent. He sat down at his desk and began to turn the pages of a book. After a long interval there came from him a quite other voice, soft, faint, deep.

"Have you ever thought about your life and what your future would be like, my dear little girl?"

"Like the future of all the girls hereabouts," Bernadette answered quickly and spontaneously.

Peyramale did not lift his eyes from the book as he continued: "You're a grown girl, a woman, then, as one might say. After first communion girls may indulge in proper pleasures. They go to dances and get to know the young fellows and have real fun. Then, please God, they marry some good chap. You're a miller's child, so you might marry a miller. Then the children come. Think of your own mother. There's more trouble than joy. But such is our mortal lot and God has given us no other. Wouldn't you like to go to dances too? Wouldn't you like to be such a woman as your mother? Tell me yourself!"

Bernadette blushed and spoke vividly: "Of course I'd like to go dancing and have a husband some day like the other girls . . ."

The giant Peyramale rose and went to the girl on his creaking shoes and laid his clenched fists on her shoulders. "Then wake up! Now! Else life is at an end for you. For you are playing with fire, O Bernadette."[3]

When I crossed the Atlantic in 1940 by clipper, we left New York bound for the Azores with a heavy load of gasoline in our tanks. We had enough gasoline on board so that if word of heavy weather should come to us even when we were well over a thousand miles at sea we could still turn back and reach New York safely. But on the pilot's charts in the instrument room there was a line drawn. It was called the point of no return. If we crossed that line we must make for the Azores whatever the weather might be. For now our supply of fuel could no longer take us back; now we must go on. The joyous

[3] P. 304.

heroism of the saints has revealed to us what it means to pass the point of no return in this life.

Søren Kierkegaard used to speak of how Joachim of Fiore at the opening of the thirteenth century had proposed his famous three stages of Christian revelation: the age of the Father until the coming of Christ, the age of the Son and of His Church, and finally in a period shortly to come after Joachim's time, the prophetic age of the Holy Spirit and of a band of pious lay spirituals who would usher it in. Kierkegaard slyly suggests that we are now in the fourth period, the age of the devil. But the devil being so busy at present has turned over the job to the professors who in their academic way are doing quite nicely at his work. Before the heroic singleness of the saint's life we find it hard to remain content with our intellectual approaches to religion, important as they may be. The saint is not a professor who puts to society a convincing set of arguments. He puts before men a life and an embarrassing invitation which they must decide to accept or reject.

With some hint of approval of the proverb that "the saint is the best theologian," Gilson in his fine study of Bonaventura, the God-child of Francis of Assisi, has written:

To know how to reach the summit of Alverna (where Francis received the stigmata) it is not enough to be able to rattle off a description of all of the roads that lead to the summit. Rather we must choose one of these roads and set our foot upon it with the firm resolution to travel it to the end.[4]

It is a callous individual or a callous society that can feel content with itself in the presence of this heroic singleness of the saint.

[4] *Bonaventura*, p. 422.

THE STAYING POWER OF THE SAINT

In the third place, the saints have revealed to society and to those who continue to call themselves Christians the persistence, the staying power of an established Christian individual. William Penn's word from the Tower, where he was imprisoned in 1669, has in it the note that governments and fellow-Christians have been compelled to recognize in the grounded Christian, "My prison shall be my grave before I will budge one jot, for I owe allegiance to no mortal man." Having received his orders from within, he is not one who can be moved when the public or the official wind changes to another quarter. The band of Quakers to which Penn had joined himself laid down its testimony on war in 1660 saying, "This is our testimony to the whole world. The Spirit of Christ by which we are guided is not changeable so as once to command us from a thing of evil and again to move us into it."

There is a toughness of fiber here that would have delighted Thoreau, who longed to have the company of men whose backbone was made of the stuff you couldn't put your hand through. There is gristle to the established Christian saint that will not yield short of his total destruction. And when he has been physically destroyed, he is still to be reckoned with.

It is this firmness in an established man that enables him to stand alone when he sees what is required of him. Joseph Hoag, in speaking to an audience in 1812 on his concern for peace, was confronted by a heckler who said. "Well stranger if all the world was of your mind, I would turn and follow after." Joseph Hoag replied, "So thou hast a mind to be the last man in the world to be good. I have a mind to be one of the first." William James in his *Varieties of Religious Experience*, commented on the significance of this firm willingness to begin, if necessary, alone: "If things are ever to move upward, someone must be ready to take the first step and to assume the risk of it."

It is this spirit of inward firmness that makes a Bernard of Clairvaux withstand all opposition and preach against the popular twelfth century persecution of the Jews; that sent Francis of Assisi on an errand to the Sultan and that kept him from being deterred by the mere fact that the Sultan was surrounded by armies who were at war with their Christian attackers; that sped Catherine of Siena on a mission to the Avignon pope, and that let nothing that appeared, whether it was the powerful French royal family, the college of cardinals, or the combined court of Avignon officials stand in the way of her completing her inward commission of persuading the pope to return and reside in Rome in order to heal the breach in Christian peace. Her comment on the Avignon period has that salty, cryptic quality of the saint, "very mysterious, very fruitful." It is this same inward galvanization that raised Woolman above dissuasion from the apparently hopeless task of combating the deeply-rooted slave system in the American colonies.

In the saints we have men and women who stand and who are not thrown off balance by opposition. It is no accident that in Germany the Roman Catholic church, in spite of its problems with the stubborn individual resistance of the saints to its iniquities in past ages, has sought by every means in its power in the last Hitler years to develop this saintly individual integrity of conscience in its members. For it saw that many of them would have to stand alone if they were to be the seed beneath the snow. To regard the witness of the saints with care is to be reminded that if the trunk of a tree catches the rock mass early, a single, firmly-rooted tree can often hold back an avalanche.

In 1937 in Western Norway near Haugesund, I met a Norwegian Quaker named Stakkland. He was the third generation of Stakklands to suffer persecution for his inner concern and to stand firmly in the face of it. His grandfather had had his farm, his animals, and even his very bedclothing sold at auction for refusing military service, tithes and official church attendance. His father had been taken from the plow and lugged off to prison for his conscientious refusal to train himself to kill in the army. His horse was left standing, and he was not even able to say good-bye to his family. Søren Stakkland had himself served a term in prison for the same conscientious stand before statutes, recognizing what these three men had maintained for a century, provided the alternative of civilian service for service in the army.

This perseverance in Christian individuals has come from their singleness of vision and from their inner renewal, when the weariness and hopelessness of their stand has often enough brought to their lips the cry of anguish, "My God, my God, why hast thou forsaken me?" Catherine of Siena, defeated and harassed on every front, wrote to a friend, "Our Saviour has placed me upon the island, and the winds beat upon me from every side." Yet, even on such an island of desolation they seem able to add the Psalmist's confident line, "I had fainted, unless I believed in the goodness of the Lord in the land of the living." And this belief so far renews them that for themselves and for their followers, they will brook no obstacle as final and no opposition as rendering what is laid upon them impossible. Catherine of Siena, true to this confidence that with God nothing is impossible, was not sparing in her lash when her trusted follower, delle Vigne, was turned back at the Italian frontier, cowed by the arrest of his companion, and gave up his mission to France. "If you could not walk there, you could have crawled; if you could not go as a friar, you could have gone as a pilgrim; if you had no money, you could have begged your way there." The saints' practice bears out the old Puritan saying that the perseverance of the saints is a continual stream of new beginnings, and for them to be thwarted on one front means only quietly to move to another. But the campaign goes on.

THE SAINT CARES NOT FOR HUMANITY BUT FOR MEN

In the fourth place, the saint really cares for his fellows, cares not abstractly but personally for others, and from the inside their needs are laid deeply upon him. Having begun with himself, the real saint never stops there. Dostoevski speaks for the saints when in *The Brothers Karamazov* he writes:

There is only one means of salvation, to make yourself responsible for other men's sins; that is the truth, you know friends, for as soon as you sincerely make yourself responsible for everything, for all men, you will see at once that it is really so, and that you are to blame for everyone and for all things. But throwing your own indolence and impatience on others, you will end by sharing the pride of Satan and murmuring against God.

Jean Frederic Oberlin slipping off his horse and onto his knees outside the little village of Ban de la Roche with scalding tears streaming down his cheeks and praying God for help in ministering to his terribly needy people; Catherine of Siena praying the night through for the souls of those in high office on whose decisions great issues for the suffering people depend, or tending an embittered leper through her ghastly last illness and then burying her, or going to the block with a doomed prisoner, or comforting in an intensely personal way each member of a little band under the persecutions which they had to bear —these are all of a piece with this infinite caring into which the great saints have been brought. Chesterton says tellingly, "St. Francis did not love humanity, but men." This caring the saints share with their brothers, the social revolutionaries, who at this point come very close to the saints. Yet, in the temptation for this brother love to become doctrinaire and abstract and to degenerate into a willingness to sacrifice any number of individuals in order to get and to keep their way, at this point the social revolutionaries are more vulnerable than the saints, to whom these same temptations are also present, but to whom they are ever bared anew in the confessional of the heart.

THE SAINT'S FAITH THAT GROUP LIFE IS REDEEMABLE

In the fifth place, the saint cuts through the lines of the sacred and profane, of the personal and the social, and regards all life as sacramental and deals with it as such. To treat group life as inevitably immoral, inaccessible to brotherhood, and unsacramental, and to accept an unbridgeable gulf between personal and group relationships after the fashion of our currently popular socio-theological pessimism, are for the saint acts of high treason. The saint's life is a witness, sometimes a silent witness and sometimes a vocal witness, against it. The saint does not arrive at his ethical insight from a study of the power ethics of mass-groups. He arrives at it from a firsthand knowledge of the power of the *I*, the *Me* and, the *Mine* in the heart of man and of the expulsive power of God's love to melt them down and to allow brotherhood to emerge. Group egotism, group pride, and group sin are all intense realities for the saint, and he knows them as a lump that is hard to reduce. But he would not let the lump-like nature of group sin intimidate him into accepting it as an ultimate and irreducible surd. God has faced lumps of corporate sin before, even lumps that were in their surroundings more coherent and more defiant than those of our day, and He has softened them up and often dissolved them. The saint knows that he does not work alone.

The Catholic saints have chosen to work from within the family of the church and to seek to save the institution even when openly or by the powerful example of their lives, they sought to restore the course of its life to the life of brotherhood in the early Christian church. This vigorous, reforming zeal in the presence of basic loyalty to the church can be widely noted. Augustine's *City of God* makes no identification of the church with the *City of God*. He is too aware that the church in his day is not alone the leaven. It has taken on too many characteristics of the loaf that it would raise to be regarded as the City of God. Benedict of Nursia fled both the worldly church and the decadent public life of his day in order to find God and to establish a way of really dedicated life to God. Yet he kept his connection with and obedience to the church unsevered. Bernard of Clairvaux gave his own life to restoring the austere simplicity of the monastic life of Europe. Francis of Assisi may have devoutly kissed the hoof prints of a priest's donkey, but he challenged the very life of the power and wealth of a swollen church and its hierarchy by his witness to the joy of a literal following of the lowly Jesus. Dean Sperry, in one of the most striking passages in his *Strangers and Pilgrims*, has said:

More often than otherwise the would-be reformers leave the settled institution in holy impatience, to become heretics and founders of schisms . . . and since schismatics are wont to rest their case upon neglected truths, they too often condemn themselves to live on half-truths. For this reason a genuine reform within a settled religious society, though far more difficult to achieve than a schism, is more effective. The utter originality of St. Francis lay in his refusal to take the path of heresy and schism. He discredited the immoralities of the church by the flank attack of a life of patent purity and rededication to Christian ideals.[5]

Catherine of Siena's loyalty to the Church Triumphant was never in question, but her denunciations and prophetic warnings against the corruptions in the church of her day never ceased until her death. To the pope's shallow efforts at reform she bluntly insists, "If you want to rebuild, you must destroy right down to the foundation." Theresa of Avila and John of the Cross spent the latter part of their lives travelling in a lumber wagon all over Spain, establishing and nursing through infancy a severely reformed Discalced Order of Carmelites against

[5] P. 146f.

every known kind of opposition from the church's hierarchy. To name a few from the Protestant group, Boehme, Fox, Woolman, Oberlin and Matilda Wrede all denounced wrong in high places and busied themselves with constructive reform.

The great Christian saints might well have had chiseled on their tombstones, if we could find them, the emblem that is borne by Ibsen's black obelisk in Oslo, a hammer. For they, too, used a hammer against the lump with great power. But beside the hammer would have to be placed the figure of a trowel. For the great Christian saints have been builders. The saint has softened the lump in more than one institution. But he has also presided over the building of a creative solution on its site. Space does not permit of the enumeration of the details of Benedict's Rule that has given a creative structure to fourteen hundred years of communistic living in Christian monasticism; of Bernard of Clairvaux's spiritual power as an arbitrator that could bring stiff-necked dukes, like Aquitaine, literally to their knees in penance, or a rival pope to a secret midnight abdication in Bernard's chambers; of Francis of Assisi's reconciliation of warring municipal factions in central Italy or of the profound stroke for good upon the social and economic life of southern Europe in the thirteenth and fourteenth centuries which his inauguration of the Franciscan Third Order effected; of Groote's holy educational mission in the creation of the Brethren of the Common Life, out of which came the pious guild of teaching brothers; or of the spiritually-grounded social innovations of Vincent de Paul, Fox, Woolman or Oberlin. Striking at the heart of these established institutional lumps, often with creative institutional innovations, these

men and women were mightily feared by the selfish vested
interests of their day, even though long after their death
those who quaked may have participated in their canoniza-
tion.

The late William Sullivan wrote in his *Epigrams and
Criticisms in Miniature* of the inwardly grounded saint:

In the one phase, he is quiet, surrendering his whole being
down to his faintest thought to an Omnipresent Glory of the
Righteous Will. In the other phase, he is militant, bringing
down his pulverizing hammer upon slippery churches, immoral
states, brutal wealth, thieving confiscations, and corrupt schools.
He is that awful apparition hated equally by potentates and
proletarians, an absolutely impartial man who will never serve
a human cause by servility, nor a divine cause by lies.

THE SAINT IS NOT INFALLIBLE

Now in all that has been said, there is no denial of the
fact that there are those who mistake being against
society for conscience, and whose claim to Christian in-
dividualism is no more than a self-admiring stubbornness.
There are also the pseudo-saints who simulate piety and
take what advantage they can from it, but whose conduct
and lack of inner mellowness and joy deceive only themselves. Every parish and every monastery has specimens of
these cadaverous and stiffly-patterned righteous ones. But
the grounded Christian individual of whom we have been
speaking is not likely to be confused in your minds with
these aberrations.

Yet, the Christian, no matter if he is in the ranks of the
real saints, is not by reason of that, infallible, and when
his judgments in regard to society are examined, this becomes very clear. He may be able to see and to act in some

area with great clarity, and in other areas he may be very much the child of his age. Professor Mecklin, in a striking sociological study entitled *The Passing of the Saint,* has drawn attention to blind areas in even the greatest saints' range of vision, such as Augustine's harsh dealings with the Donatist heretics or Bernard of Clairvaux's persecution of the small heretical peasant sects in southern France, his championing of an abortive crusade and his firm dealing with Abelard at the Council of Sens. Francis of Assisi's abdication of the headship of his order on his return from the Holy Land in 1219, paving the way for the heavy hand of Father Elias and the orthodox monastic party and for the repression of the spiritual Franciscans, has long troubled those of us who know and love him. If we look at Catherine of Siena's specific political missions, they are an unbroken record of failure except for her restoration of the pope in Rome, which at his death resulted in a schism. William Penn spent almost a year in a debtor's prison in London over financial troubles that came about through his trust in a corrupt steward, and in the year of his death, 1718, his famous, lenient penal code in Pennsylvania, which he set such store by and believed he had firmly anchored, was completely set aside in favor of the full British set of vicious penal statutes. Anyone who claims infallible wisdom or strategy for the saints in all social and political areas only does so because he is ignorant of the facts.

Yet, when this has been admitted, it does not set aside the saint's influence on society in specific areas where his vision did cut through conventional wrappings to the issue itself, nor does it affect the contribution which his living a full life in response to man's highest calling makes upon the generation.

HOW MAY THE SAINT INFLUENCE SOCIETY?

Aldous Huxley's *Grey Eminence* in which a brilliant and devout monk, Father Joseph, is depicted as being drafted directly into making the political decisions of Richelieu's administration, including the nefarious prolonging of the Thirty Years' War in order for France to gain by the ruin of her enemies, has sharply raised the issue of the reason why so many saintly men who put their hand on government, whether it be ecclesiastical or political, become simply cogs in the machine and lose all moral influence upon it. Huxley's solution that in Father Joseph's case it was due to his false method of meditation, in which this Capuchin monk fixated himself on the crucified and suffering Christ, will satisfy but few. For there are too many others whose meditations have not been of this type who have suffered a similar impotence. Does this mean, then, that the saint should never accept administrative responsibility, that there is something so evil in all institutional systems as such, that they must corrupt all they touch? Does it mean that he is powerless to heal such monsters and that he can never expect to produce social, but only individual and personal, mutations? This is the conclusion of a man like Olaf Stapleton in his *Saints and Revolutionaries* when, believing the saint to be indispensable to any creative revolution, he still declares:

Most ordinary saints are quite unequipped for politics. And I doubt whether even with good equipment the ordinary saint who is not exceptionally shrewd can ever be a wholehearted and effective revolutionary. Vivid consciousness of the fundamental humanity of all men, even of the enemies of the revolution, is apt to snare him into being tolerant and conciliatory when he should be firm. On the other hand, a revolution in which the saints exercise no influence is sure to degenerate sooner or later into a ruthless tyranny.[6]

Gerald Heard has suggested a counselling arrangement between actual administration and the saint that resembles the system of the Elder Statesman in Japan, who, although living a life of complete retirement, is yet visited and consulted before any final decision was reached on matters of great moment to the states, and who after delivering himself with unusual terseness, left both the responsibility for the final decision and the administration of it upon the active ministers of the state.

There is in this suggestion, however, a kind of religious specialization which can scarcely satisfy those who accept the claim that all life is sacramental and that even institutions as frozen forms of brotherhood are not impervious to redemption although the process is slower and infinitely more costly than that of redeeming a single individual. Repeated experiences have made all too clear the negative side of this conclusion, namely, that when leaders and followers who have not been saved from themselves project their panaceas into existence, we get only demonic and bastard types of social salvation.

To refuse the responsibility of direct administration if called to it, however, has not been the saint's way, and scarcely a man or a woman that we have mentioned here has not held some onerous administrative office and for all of the fallible traits has revealed great faithfulness and effectiveness at the task. It has been one of the acts of

[6] P. 32.

genius of the Roman Catholic church to harness its saints. The actual institutional mutations, the new patterns of brotherhood that they have created or reformed or refashioned: the Augustinian, Benedictine, Cistercian, Franciscan orders and especially the Third Order Franciscans, the hospitals and houses for widows and unmarried women, the Brethren of the Common Life Schools, the barefoot Carmelites, the original State of Pennsylvania, the pattern for voluntarily freeing the slaves, these are significant corporate mutations. But they are not significant enough. And the actual forms of brotherhood of our modern world are too little influenced by them, and too much under the influence of institutions that have come from another wave-length. The saint of the future may not be able to avoid the cross of personally creating new community patterns in his attempt to offer himself and his fellows without reservation to God.

The saint's contribution to specific corporate mutations, however, must ever be second to his direct influence upon society through his own striking faithfulness to something that transcends society. This witness to an order impinging upon ours but never realized here is a perpetual threat to society's idolatrous attempt to set itself up as the exclusive object of worship—the golden calf of its time. Here is a gay, joyous, strong soul that has no price, that cannot be bought. So long as staunch, devoted Christian individuals remain, there is at work in society a powerful force to reassert the principle of order and to compel the state or any social institution to consider its relation to the true end of individual men. Thoreau's insistence that "there will never be a really free and enlightened state until the state comes to recognize the individual as a higher and independent power from which all its own power and authority are derived" is a poignant and valuable observation. But it puts the emphasis at the wrong point when it seeks to limit the big unit by reminding it that it is only an aggregate of little units. The state or any other large unit will never be checked on any such quantitative terms. It is a question of the dream, of the ideal, of the ultimate purpose of man. Establish that, and exemplify it in living specimens that can outlive, outlove, and outdie those whose lives are governed by a lesser end, specimens that can reveal not "bargains in brotherhood" but brotherhood as Francis revealed it in his comradeship of suffering with the poor, and the institution is attacked at its vulnerable core where it, too, must continually vindicate and renew itself or finally perish and be replaced.

It is here that the saint, that the devoted Christian individual exerts his full power, for he incarnates the dream and lifts the whole level of faithfulness. Franz Werfel has revealed in the Preface of his *Song of Bernadette* what he regards to be his task as a writer:

Even in the days when I wrote my first verses, I vowed that I would evermore and everywhere in all I wrote magnify the divine mystery and holiness of man, careless of a period which has turned with scorn and rage and indifference from the ultimate values of our moral lot.

This, although he is usually quite unconscious of it, is exactly what the saint by his life of intense devotion to Christ and his fellow man does for any period; he "magnifies the divine mystery and holiness of man." His life is a transfusion of fresh blood into the blood stream of society.

They come to us from the country of truth . . . after the Greatest Witness who has revealed to us the Father . . . they may say in the word of the Beloved Disciple, "That which we have seen, that which we have heard, that which our hands have handled declare we unto you!" And our souls quiver with hope and longing to hear what they have to tell. Witnesses are they to the Gracious Presence of God in humanity.

In the valley below the beautiful hill on which the city of Assisi perches snugly and securely is to be found the little chapel which the Benedictines generously gave to Francis and his first companions for worship. It was in this *Portiuncula* as they affectionately called it that Francis got the rule for the order from the reading of the missal one morning, and he always looked on this little chapel as the spiritual cradle of his gallant band. Today a great church, St. Mary of the Angels, has been built over the *Portiuncula*. From all outward appearances it is clear that it is this vast and imposing St. Mary of the Angels that shelters and protects this crude little chapel. But a more discerning view would show that this great church owes not only its very existence but also the lure that brings millions of visitors to worship in it to this tiny shell that stands in its midst. Society in a moment of sudden awareness of its debt to the saint might some day repeat Gorky's words of gratitude, spoken of Tolstoy, "I am not an orphan on earth so long as this man lives on it."

CHAPTER II

THE AUTHORITY OF THE SAINT

I BELIEVE that what the religious life of the world needs most of all is not a new theology, not a vast new crop of brilliant students as candidates for the ministry, not a union of all sects into one religious body, not a renewed missionary movement, not a revised program of evangelism. What it needs first and foremost is apostles or saints, men and women prepared to live in the full dispensation of Christian freedom.

What is an "apostle," or if you like, a "saint"? Either term is so alien to our ordinary habits of thought that it needs definition and clarification and illustration. If a "saint" or an "apostle" were defined as a religious genius, the modern mind would be better able to understand it. In fact, John Middleton Murry did seek to commend his study of Jesus to the modern mind by calling it *Jesus, Man of Genius*. Now a genius is an exaggerated type. He has an ordinary man's gifts in extraordinary quantity. As if by accident or by a mutation, nature seems to have spilled into one person gifts of intellect, will, or emotion that might ordinarily have done for several men. This excess of gifts enables him to enjoy the luxury of a brilliant self-sufficiency. He can almost live off the interest on his capital. Genius is a gift; no effort will produce it. It is the possession of a few and so is not likely to upset the social laws that are geared to the ordinary man's capacities. There are exceptions to every law, and it can be accommodated to include them. The ordinary man need not feel challenged by the presence of the genius. There is nothing either he or the genius can do about it. These exceptions can be praised, honored, supported, and if they turn out to be unpleasant, they can be avoided except when the common man may find he can make use of the services of the genius.

GENIUS AND RELIGION AS A MATTER OF TASTE OR TEMPERAMENT

It is a common assumption today that religion in general is a matter of personal feeling or taste, just as music, art, or literature. Some seem to have a gift for it. Others get on very well without it. Some are naturally religious; others can find no place for it in their lives. It is suggested that some have a high and some a low emotional quotient, that some are born Platonists and mystics, others Aristotelians and hard-headed realists. Or it is sometimes suggested that it may be a matter of psychological type, the introvert perhaps favoring religion and the extrovert finding little of interest in it.

The logical conclusion to this is too obvious to need drawing. If the Christian religion is a matter of taste, of emotional quotient, of psychological type, and if I do not have that feeling or that emotional temperament or am not that type, then I may conclude that it has nothing for me, and that ends the matter. It is quite in keeping with this modern temper, therefore, to accept the apostle or the saint as a genius and to give him a niche in the public pantheon along with the specimens of genius in other fields. An elective course might even be given on the saints in one of our broad-minded modern universities, as has been done for the general subject of religion.

But if the apostle or saint, as apostle or saint, is not a genius, if the very nature of apostleship or sainthood is in radical contradiction with the modern's conception of a genius, if the apostle or the saint wields an authority that refuses this offer of tolerance, if, scenting its real purpose the saint refuses this gracious offer to be raised from the Commons to the House of Lords where he may never be prime minister of the Commons, then the real character of an apostle may emerge, and emerge with such clarity that even a modern eye cannot evade it.

Now, an "apostle" is not an apostle by reason of any inherited characteristics either of physique, intelligence, will, emotion, psychological type, or abnormal faculty of mystical apprehension. He is an apostle only as whatever capacities he possesses are wholly open to use for the purposes of God. He is an apostle by reason of the totality of his abandonment to God. He is an apostle because the supernatural world that impinges upon the natural has become real enough to reckon on in every calculation of life. An apostle is "just a human being released from the love of self and enslaved by the love of God," and he rejoices in it. The life of an apostle is one where "God and His eternal order have more and more their undivided sway." The only difference between an apostle and ourselves is that he has faced and accepted without condition the quiet demand, "Who chooseth me must give and hazard all he hath," and we have not. A wag has suggested that a moderately good Christian is about as good as a moderately good egg. In an apostle we see exemplified the profound truth of the old maxim that if you want to be good, you must be heroically good.

THE AUTHORITY OF AN APOSTLE

From what source does an apostle derive the authority which makes itself felt on those who meet him? It is clear that the apostle's authority does not spring from his native cleverness, or the richness of his phantasy life, or the brilliance of his powers of expression, as they do in the genius. Nor is the apostle's authority dependent alone upon the way he lives. "That he lives according to his teaching," wrote Søren Kierkegaard, "is no proof of his rightness. It might better be said that he lives according to his teaching because he is convinced of its rightness."

The authority of an apostle actually comes from the character and ground of his *being* that man feels in him. He has been sufficiently ordered and simplified and gotten out of the way so that the power and authority of God makes itself felt through him. "People ought to be less concerned about what they ought to do and more concerned about what they ought to be," declared Meister Eckhart in one of his tractates. "For if they were good, and their dispositions were good, then good works would shine forth brightly."[1] It is this *being* and the sense of this *being's* speaking through an apostle that vest him with spiritual authority. Because of this, the authority of the apostle is felt as much in repose as in action, as much in his presence and concern as in his speech, as much in the ripeness of great age as at the height of his powers.

Men did not seem to be able to remember what Francis

[1] *Sermons-Tractates*, C. de B. Evans translation, Vol. II, p. 6.

of Assisi said in his sermons. Yet, after he preached, whole villages begged to be allowed to join his order. Reading the sermons of the Curé of Ars, one cannot understand what laid some of the ablest minds in France under his spell. Yet, crowds waited for days to enter his confessional. The aged and enfeebled John, when he was only able to say, "Little children, love one another," melted congregations. The authority of the genius, on the other hand, remains only so long as he preserves his cleverness. When George Bernard Shaw's satirical cleverness fades, his authority vanishes.[2]

THE CLAIM OF THE APOSTLE UPON EVEN THE GENIUS

Now the life of a genius is restricted to the few. The life of the apostle is open to all and lays its claim upon all. And it is the apostle's insistence upon this issue that rejects point-blank the pleasant tolerance of the modern temper. Harry Emerson Fosdick tells of a Roman Catholic priest coming up to minister to a wounded soldier in the last war. The soldier said to him, "Thanks just the same, Padre, but I don't belong to your church."

"I know," said the padre, and he spoke like an apostle, "but you belong to my God."

[2] Søren Kierkegaard, in a remarkable essay on *Apostle and Genius*, goes further and hints that the genius's authority comes in part from the newness of what he says. He by his added gifts has stolen a march and gotten hold of a truth, and like a columnist has given an advance tip. It is like telling a joke— if others have not heard it, you get credit for being the first to tell it. After others have heard it, you get no credit. When the masses assimilate what the genius has told them, the message will lose its novelty; and he, his authority. Just as a teacher is no longer an authority for a pupil who surpasses him in knowledge, so with the authority of the genius. The authority of the genius, then, is only a temporary authority, gained by his anticipating the times. The authority of the apostle, however, remains when the truth of what he announces is fully understood by others.

There is a kind of echo of the words, "Ye have not chosen me, but I have chosen you," in the claim of the apostle upon the lives of every man and woman that has ever come into the world. And the authority of the apostle or saint makes this claim felt in all he meets, as no intellectual argument could ever do. For the universal God-man that speaks in the apostle has an invisible ally in the breast of every man, no matter how deeply concealed or repudiated it may be. William Law describes this Trojan horse that we bear within us and that will betray us to our good when he says, "Man has a seed of the Divine life given unto the birth of his soul, a seed that has all the riches of eternity in it and is always wanting to come to birth in him and be alive in God." George Fox says, "In every man there is something that is not of dust or earth or flesh or time, but of God." It is to this that the authority of the apostle speaks as he follows Fox's instruction "to walk joyfully over the earth answering to that of God in every man."

Since the life of an apostle is open to all, a genius may become an apostle, but not as genius. When the brilliant desert-explorer, Charles Foucauld, a hero of all France by the age of twenty-seven, came to the Abbé Huvelin's little church and, finding the Abbé in the confessional, asked him to step out for a visit about his condition of soul, the Abbé quietly but firmly told him to enter the confessional, to get down on his knees like the humblest peasant, and to make his confession. He obeyed, and out of what broke through there, came one of the most moving religious spirits of the last century. A distinguished Frenchman came to see the Curé of Ars while he was hearing confessions. The old Curé pointed to the stool where penitents usually knelt. "M. le Curé," the man hastened to say politely, "I have not come to make my confession, but to discuss things with you."

The Curé replied, "Oh my friend, you have come to the wrong place; I have no skill at discussion. But if it is consolation that you want, kneel there, where many have knelt before you and have not regretted it."

"But M. le Curé, you are asking me to act on utter force."

"Kneel there."

He knelt, made the sign of the cross, and began his confession. He arose, not only comforted, but believing. This is not alone the authority of the Roman Catholic Church. Like Huvelin's, it was the authority of an apostle who no longer acted simply of himself. Apart from this inner authority, these commands are just absurd, just funny, to a genius.

Take away the passion and conviction by which they always live, the passion for God, the conviction of the absolute priority of the Eternal, and the vivid presence and ceaseless pressure of God with the world . . . Take away this which is the whole meaning of his life, and the saint looks insignificant and often rather silly too.[3]

The demands that Huvelin and the Curé of Ars made upon their distinguished visitors were of a piece with the demands apostleship always makes upon genius. For only as he, the genius, with his exceptional powers of intellect and will and emotion and phantasy—powers that enable him to see all around the question, powers that enable him to find a thousand most impressive reasons for retaining

[3] Evelyn Underhill, *Mixed Pasture*, p. 149.

their autonomy, powers that are often, like Nietzsche's camel symbol, laden with the freight of ancient wisdom— only as the genius becomes vulnerable, becomes as a little child, passes under the piercing gaze of the all-loving One, who melts down all the hidden arrogance, only then does the genius become an apostle. Only as that piercing gaze discovers to him his need—how he is only one among many, how he, along with every other needy soul that has ever come into the world, through every moment of his life has been singled out and loved with a personal passion and concern, how only as he has begun to love back with every pore of his being can he do that for which he was made—only then does the genius become an apostle.

In 1926 Anker Larsen, a brilliant Danish novelist, wrote in an autobiographical fragment, *With the Door Open*:

When God entered into my life, warm and powerful, it was from them [the farm laborers on the great Danish farms he had known as a boy] that I learned my right relationship to Him. "No more, therefore, than Thou wilt, and not for my sake, but for the sake of that which thou intendest for me." In this I saw the crux of my situation. I resolved to renounce personal aims; I tried to "sell all I possessed" and to enter the service of the Great Farmer, to report to him merrily in the morning with the question, "What orders have you got for me today?"

IS THE APOSTLE AN ANTI-INTELLECTUALIST?

In emphasizing how the genius like the simplest peasant must go beyond self and the tools of self in order to enter the service of the Great Farmer, in order to become an apostle, there is no plunge into a blind anti-intellectualism that is implied in this claim of the saints. It is true that the

Imitation of Christ contains passages such as "At the last day of judgment you shall not be examined upon how much you have read, but upon how well you have lived." And Pascal in *Thoughts* places the order of charity above the order of sense and even above the order of the intellect and insists that in man "there is an infinite abyss that can only be filled by an infinite and immutable object," i.e., by God, who alone can draw a man up into this third order of charity in which our true salvation consists. Yet these claims are insolent not to the intellect but only to the egotism of the intellect. Groote and Pascal were among the most brilliant intellects of their countries in the respective centuries in which they lived. But they knew, also, that until the intellect had found and yielded to its ground, its root, its principle, until the abyss in man had been filled, the intellect could never be relied upon to bring men into the true freedom for which he seems by his nature to be designed. In the service of the new center Groote and Pascal have been free to use their intellects with an uncanny power and effectiveness, as one who knows Groote's *Imitation of Christ*, which Thomas à Kempis gave to the world, or the *Provincial Letters* or the *Thoughts* of Pascal can testify all too well. The revised estimate of the arrogant ungrounded intellect in an apostle who has come to know that which grounds and completes and orders the intellect must never be confused with the cheap anti-intellectualism of those who have never even fathomed the mind's own powers. What the saint would emphasize is that if the intellect's passion for autonomy, its private egotism, is a barrier to a man's discovery of his life purpose and of the active relating of his life to God, as it frequently is, then, like the offending eye or hand, it had better be plucked out or cut off than that a man should be capsuled up in an effort at autonomy which is doomed to bring about ultimate frustration and the atrophy of his being. "*Reason* is not sin," says the seventeenth-century Quaker mystic, Isaac Pennington, "but a deviation from that place from which reason came, is sin."

THE APOSTLE'S CLAIM ON EVERY TYPE OF MAN

Further, the saint would point out that apostleship was the way for *every* life, no matter what its gifts of intellect or will or emotion, for the one-talent man as well as for the ten-talent man, and that it mattered not at all to God whether the gift of himself that the apostle lays at the crèche was a wisp of wool brought by a shepherd or a great skein of golden thread brought by a rich king. God could use them both and weave them into the tapestry of His design for living. The saint's insistence has been that apostleship can begin at any time, with any capacities. It matters not at all where it begins or with what; but it matters most of all what begins to happen then, how these native capacities over the years are drawn together into a unique life, and how the noose of God tightens over these capacities and connections with which a man entered this life and pulls them together as He draws this individual on into the joyous agony of cocreation with Him.

Augustine in one of his sermons puts it well:

God is over all men, and yet somehow or other one does not easily dare to say *My* God, except he believes in Him and loves Him; then he says *My* God . . . The rich man Zaccheus gave away the half of his goods that he might attain to God (Luke 19:8); that he might so attain, Peter left his nets and ship (Matt. 4:20); that she might attain, the poor widow gave her two mites (Luke 21:2); that a still poorer person might attain, he held out a cup of cold water (Matt. 10:42); and one who was utterly poor and needy proffered only good will that he might attain (Luke 15:14). These gave diverse things but they all attained to Him, because they did not love diverse things . . . some in honor, others without honor; some with money, others without money; some fair of body, others less fair; some tired with age, others in the vigor of youth; some of them boys, others grown men or women—God is equally present to all . . . O happy we, with such a possession, such a Possessor . . . straightway with all the sweetness of thy affection, and with sure and utterly trustful love, say, *My* God.[4]

As we look over Christian history, we see that the makings of an apostle may be in a vacillating Peter; a mystically-minded John; an authoritarian Jewish law-giver, Paul; strong, passionate, willful dispositions like those of Tertullian, Augustine, and Pascal; eclectic, balanced, rational natures like Clement of Alexandria, and Origen, Aquinas and Erasmus; poets and minnesingers like Francis of Assisi and Jacopone da Todi, Henry Suso, Thomas Traherne and Francis Thompson; difficult personalities with naturally fragile and often disrupted psycho-physical dispositions, such as those of Catherine of Genoa, Theresa of Avila, or Søren Kierkegaard; a mother of many children and an eminently practical administrator like Bridget of Sweden; a German cobbler, Boehme; an English leatherworker, Fox; a New Jersey tailor, Woolman; an illiterate French peasant who could not pass his theological examinations and was so particularly deficient in moral theology that it was thought wise for years not to trust him to hear confessions, the Curé of Ars. This is what the apostle means when he says that the Christian religion is not for

[4] *Sermons*, XLVII, xvi, 30.

geniuses or specialists or people of one peculiar temperament or class or taste or capacity, but is for all. What
you bring does not matter, provided you bring all of it.

HOW THE NOOSE OF GOD DRAWS THE LIFE OF AN APOSTLE INTO CREATIVENESS

There is, however, a strong resistance, a kind of willful
negativism, on the part of most of our minds that makes
them deny that the apostles began where we are now and
that it was not *what* they brought but *where they are
brought to* that is of real importance. For once this ad-
mission is made, it strips from us another excuse, another
cloak of evasion, and makes us more vulnerable to the
claim of apostleship. It is, therefore, of first importance in
understanding the nature of an apostle to see what growth
has occurred in him from the time of his entry into the life
of apostleship to his passing from this life. There have
been richly-gifted natures that could by their endowments
alone have commanded prestige and position and ad-
miration.

A Philadelphia Friend said of Rebecca Jones (Bouncing
Bett), a handsome, brilliant, vivacious Quaker woman of
the late eighteenth century, "It was well that she bowed to
the conviction of truth in her early days, for she would
have been a most powerful instrument in His Satanic
Majesty's band."

Sir Thomas More was a strong, brilliant, witty, lovable
fellow who might have been that and nothing more. He
might well have become a scholar, a great barrister, a
courtier of Henry the Eighth, or a social reformer. In
fact he did become all of these and infinitely more. But
from the days of his living with the Carthusians as a young

law student, this genius of his generation came under holy obedience, and his deliberate choice of remaining in the world, of marriage and a family, of a career at law and letters, was all brought to this new focus. He wore each of these vocations as you and I might wear a coat, now of this weave and now of that. But secretly, beneath these garments he wore a shirt of hair, just as a reminder of his tryst. Because of his inward vocation that lay under them all, he wore these outer garments lightly, with abandon, and when the inward vocation drew him to refuse his acquiescence in Henry the Eighth's willful dealing with the matter of his second wife and with the church, More could lay off these outer vocations with a quiet contentment and go to his beheading with a kind of inner merriness that insulted all who did not know its cause.

Then there have been the difficult personalities who were by their heredity and upbringing marked out to suffer from the shocks of the world. Of Catherine of Genoa, von Hügel in his exhaustive study of her in the *Mystical Element of Religion* wrote, referring to her congenital defect:

A great self-engrossment of a downrightly selfish kind, a grouping of all things around such a self-adoring ego; a noiseless but determined elimination from her life and memory of all that would not or could not, then and there, be drawn and woven into the organism and functioning of this immensely self-seeking, infinitely woundable and wounded; endlessly self-doctoring "I" and "Me"; a self intensely, although not sexually jealous, envious and exacting, incapable of easy accommodation of pleasure in half successes, incapable of humor and brightness, of joyous, once-born creatureliness—all this was

certainly to be found, in strong tendency at least, in the un-
trained parts and periods of her character and life.[5]

Into the life of this sufferer, of this congenitally melancholy temperament there came the way of apostleship so
that von Hügel, surveying her life as a whole, could say
of what had happened as the noose drew tight:

If the tests of reality in such things are their persistence and
large and rich spirituality and fruitfulness, then something
profoundly real and important took place in the soul of that
sad and weary woman of twenty-six . . . Her four years of
heroic persistence; her unbroken hospital service for a quarter
of a century; her lofty magnanimity towards her husband,
her profound influence on Vernazzo in urging him on to his
splendid labours throughout Italy and to his grand death in
plague stricken Genoa, her daringly original yet immensely
persuasive doctrine . . .

These are all the fruits of decades of growth in apostleship that drew this loosely-knit and weak psycho-physical
disposition into one who could endure heavy work and
responsibility and who, while she was never wholly sound,
was so integrated from within as to be able to reveal the
power of God and to influence a wide circle about her.

Søren Kierkegaard, the Danish religious author and
prophet of the last century, introverted by nature, robbed
of a child's childhood, infected with the melancholy of his
father's sin, breaking his engagement with Regina Olsen,
yet found and lived in his vocation. How he was drawn
from the self-absorbed intensity of his early aestheticism
where debauchery, suicide, insanity, or apostleship seemed
the only alternatives for his life, into his vocation, where
gradually he was steadied, released, and held together for

[5] Vol. II, p. 37.

his writing, is another witness to the power of apostleship to transform unpromising materials into a life that is a tool in the hand of God. I have written of him elsewhere:

He found in his writing a form of worship of God, and in the exercise of his calling as a writer whose every page was composed as under the scrutiny of God, he found his healing. If one is as weak as he is and has so much to do, he will soon learn what it is to pray, he suggests. And he describes his vocation as a writer as literally living with God as one lives with a father. He rises in the morning and gives thanks to God. Then work begins. At a set time in the evening he breaks off and again gives thanks to God. Then sleep. So he lives. The twelve-hour day of writing, when his production was at its height, is broken only by a midday walk among the common people in the Østergade. This keeping of sorrow and remorse silently between oneself and God keeps a man humble and acutely aware of the service he owes to God. Buried in this center, these sufferings release light that has no fear of darkness. And rarely in religious literature has suffering been treated with such delicacy and penetration as in Kierkegaard's own writings.[6]

Not psychological peculiarities, but what von Hügel calls *perennial freshness*, a quality of being able to become more humble, true, and loving, has always been the mark of apostleship in the writings of the great apostles. And instead of pointing to the psychological peculiarities that remain in the lives of some of these sufferers who have joined the diverse ranks of the saints and apostles, I am increasingly drawn to exclaim: "See what God has done with them. Think where they might have been. Think what has been done in spite of the material."

[6] *Purity of Heart*, Introduction, p. xxiv.

Then there are the simple ones like Brother Juniper, who, in spite of Lawrence Housman's glorification of him, required long months and years to grasp what Francis was at; or Brother Lawrence, whom perfumed and laced lady-parishioners love to hold up for prompt emulation to their maids as the saint of the holy kitchen, unaware that, as he tells us, it took ten years of desolations even after entering the convent in middle life before the real practice of the presence of God emerged into his life; or a young man I have known for more than ten years, who, with no conspicuous intellectual and physical and emotional equipment, by a steadily deepening commitment at each step, as layer after layer of what he held important has been stripped off him by life, has become a remarkable influence on people of all classes who come to know him. He was in a work camp several years ago where a group of rather brilliant students and young professional people spent eight weeks at hard manual work. Their fierce intellectual and personal divisions threatened to destroy the camp. Through it all the quiet unassuming steadiness of this chap who in native intelligence, native attractiveness, in education, and in capacity to express himself was probably the least of them all, was generally acknowledged to have been the influence that drew the camp together again. Once more, it is the long period on the anvil that has hammered and drawn these simple people into tongs that God can use.

GOD'S USE OF APOSTLES

The use to which they have been put has frequently been very different from what either the apostle or the world expected, and very different from the natural inclination of either. Apostles have to learn what Tyrrell wrote von Hügel about von Hügel's unintended bad handling of his daughter, Gertrude: "God has often to undo all our work for Him and build it up again His own way." How well this applies to willful careers and fiercely-adhered-to programs and prompt answers to calls to "wider spheres of usefulness," as clergymen often refer to an opportunity to get a more prominent and distinguished post! Augustine, burning to use his native gifts of thought and writing, found himself first Bishop Coadjutor and then for the rest of his life the Bishop of the provincial diocese of Hippo on the North African coast, charged with heavy duties of preaching, administration, and even laborious service as an ecclesiastical magistrate. For thirty-five years all of his writing was done either incidental to or in the hours he snatched from these duties.

Bernard of Clairvaux, longing for the life of retirement, study and contemplation, became the spiritual and temporal counsellor of Western Europe. Harassed and worn, with almost no time to himself, compelled to travel much and able to write his meditations only in intervals where illness had immobilized him or in sermons like those in the *Canticle of Canticles* which he preached to his monks whenever he was at Clairvaux, Bernard came to know how different is the life of an apostle from what he expected. As a young man, with twenty-nine of his friends and relatives, he had entered the faltering little group of reformist Benedictines called the Cistercian Order, bent on finding an austere, balanced life of monastic retirement where he could serve God in prayer and manual labor. Having left the world, he found himself hurled into it once more, bent on its healing.

Francis of Assisi, in 1209, longing by natural inclination to take up the life of an Umbrian hermit and to give himself up to retired prayer, is moved out into the service of preaching from which he was never again allowed to retire for long. Gerard Groote, the Dutch Apostle, arousing fourteenth-century Holland as no other voice had done by his lay preaching, is suddenly silenced when the Bishop revokes his lay-license to preach and is compelled to retire to his home at Deventer. Dante is driven from Florence into exile. The Franciscan movement, the *Spiritual Diary* of Gerard Groote (that we now believe forms the *Imitation of Christ*), and the *Divine Comedy* were the results.

It would be difficult to find a more perfect catalogue of every normal human inclination and public expectation than that addressed by Dame More in a letter to her husband, Thomas More, in the Tower where he lay for his refusal to commend Henry the Eighth's conduct:

I marvel that you that have been always hitherto taken for so wise a man will now so play the fool to lie here in this close, filthy prison, and be content thus to be shut up amongst mice and rats, when you might be abroad at your liberty and with the favor and good will both of the King and his Council, if you would but do as all the bishops and best learned in the realm have done. And seeing you have at Chelsea a right fair house, your library, your books, your gallery, your garden, your orchard, and all other necessaries so handsome about you where you might in company of me your wife, your children and household so merry, I muse what in God's name you mean here thus fondly to tarry.

More's best reply, showing that he had learned what apostleship exacts, came at his execution, where a chronicle sent to Paris describing the scene records:

He spoke little before his execution. Only he asked his by-
standers to pray for him in this world, and he would pray for
them elsewhere. He then begged them earnestly to pray for
the King, that it might please God to give him good counsel,
protesting that he died the King's good servant, but God's
first.[7]

John Woolman, when he made his first refusal to write
a will that provided for the transfer of slaves in a little
shop in Mt. Holly, New Jersey, had little intimation how
his life would be trimmed and shaped for that service, the
thousands of miles he would tramp and ride, the months
and years he would spend. The dream, toward the end of
his life, of his being so mixed with a gray mass of suffering
humanity that he could no longer reply to his own name
when he was called was a symbol of the way his life
was molded and fashioned beyond any expectation.

The procession continues: the Curé of Ars spending
sixteen to seventeen hours a day in the confessional, lying
down to rest at nine or ten in the evening and up again at
one in the morning, not wanting to disappoint the line of
waiting pilgrims who came to receive his counsel, trying to
run away from Ars again and again into a place where he
might give himself to contemplation, but always brought
back to his minute post and to the divinely-ordained
slavery to human need; the incurable sufferer committed
to the Eternal and discovering the truth of Eckhart's word
that "the swiftest animal that bears thee to thy good is
suffering"; the person left at the same work year after year,
not doing different things but now doing them differently
and for different reasons; the present Archbishop of Sweden drawn from a New Testament chair at Lund and,

[7] Chambers, *Thomas More*, p. 349.

before that, from a little church he was serving in southern Sweden—by inclination retiring, simple, at home in the small parish in intimate association with people—losing fourteen pounds in two months in trying to decide whether to accept the archbishop's post previously held by the famous and brilliant Nathan Söderblom, accepting and being today blessedly occupied in his quiet, humble way in the direction of this important office.

THE APOSTLE'S LIFE IS THE FULL HUMAN LIFE

Cromwell cried out again and again, "It is a terrible thing to fall into the hands of the living God." For the customary ambitions, expectations, and wise precautions, the lives of the apostles as we see them all bear witness to the shattering and scarification and kneading and re-kneading of the life that goes on. An apostle must be teachable. *There is death to be dealt to vast areas of claim-fulness in the apostle's life. Yet where there is no death there can be no resurrection.* And as layer after layer of this hull is broken away, these apostles testify universally not to the pain but to the joy of their way of life, and the Roman Catholic Church never canonizes a saint who has not shown this joy, this merriness in his life.

These apostles have in the end done what they wanted to do. "In my whole life I never made a sacrifice," declared David Livingstone. Matilda Wrede, the angel of the Finnish prisoners, the daughter of the governor of a province of Finland, who from the age of nineteen had given herself to the prisoners of Finland, gone up into the northern wastes of Finland to visit their families, travelled with them a part of the long journey when they were being transported to Siberia, spent her years in visits to their cells in the principal prisons in Finland, worn herself out in their service, in 1927, a few days before her death, asked her companion, "Has anyone in this generation had such a joyful life as I?"

The life of the apostle is the full life. It is not a mutilation; Søren Kierkegaard could say of what happened to his own gifts when he came under divine governance, "If one can compare intellectual talents to a stringed instrument, I may say that not only was I not out of tune, but I acquired an extra string to my instrument."

In the Franciscan Order, when a man entered the order, he gave away his property if he had any, but he kept the tools of his trade. In apostleship the individual and the racial and temperamental tools of the person are kept, for there are no two saints or apostles who are alike. Schamoni, in a lifelong scholarly study devoted to recovering the portraits of the official Catholic saints, published in Germany in 1938 an illustrated volume on *The True Visage of the Saints*. The most striking feature of the volume is to see the utterly different facial types represented. The natural tools of their heredity have indeed been retained, but the tools are now employed in a new service, and the universal and common element of apostleship is the common yielding to the Divine poultice and the willingness to be drawn into what von Hügel calls "the deepest kind of life." In a letter he wrote to George Tyrrell in 1889, he said of this life of apostleship:

The primary function of religion is not the consoling of the natural man as it finds him, but the purification of this man by effecting an ever-growing cleavage and contrast between his bad, false self and the false, blind self-love that clings to that self, and the true enlightened self-love that clings to the true self; and the confused and dumb aspirations of every human heart correspond exactly to, and come from precisely the same source as the external helps and examples of miracle, church, or saint. The truly exceptional is thus never the queer, but it is the supremely normal, and but embodies in an exceptional degree the deepest and hence exceptional longings of us all.[8]

It is because they embody the deepest and most exceptional longings in us all, because their commitment wounds and draws at these heroic longings which not even the heart of a genius can still, that the saints and apostles speak with such authority, strike at our lives, menace our lethargic torpor, and prepare us to let God work.

[8] *Von Hügel and Tyrrell*, p. 31.

CHAPTER III

A NEW SET OF DEVOTIONAL EXERCISES

IT MAY be easier to distinguish an apostle from a genius, or to indicate a few of the points where the life of the saint touches the vulnerable center of society than it is to undertake to set forth the kind of education of the will which is involved in the cultivation of the life of apostleship. Professor C. C. J. Webb is not the first to comment on the poverty of first-class religious writing in this field of the nurture of the religious life in England and America. But his diagnosis of the cause of this poverty is a novel one. He once suggested to me that English and American writers on religious subjects were so engaged at the controversial frontiers of religion, trying to defend the very existence of any Christian faith at all from the challenge of interpreters of the physical sciences, the all-engulfing secularism, and the rival class and racial religions of our time, that their energies were spent before they ever got to a consideration of the cultivation of the life of the Christian religion itself. I have sometimes thought that it is a situation that repeats the tragedy of William Penn, who, in the thirty active years of his life that followed his securing the charter for his Holy Experiment in Pennsylvania, spent twenty-five of them in England trying to keep his colony from being confiscated, and only four scant years in the actual resident nurture of the colony that cried out for his counsel and personal guidance.

The result of this neglect has been that, outside of Roman Catholic circles, there is almost no serious study and writing on what has classically been called "ascetic theology." And for the most part the want of study and writing in these fields is not an unfair index of the level of devotional practice in this large non-Catholic group.

Now there are many in liberal Protestant circles who would hail this condition of a lack of attention to specifically devotional practices as a welcome emancipation from the self-conscious concern of the Middle Ages and of the Counter-Reformation with the search for personal salvation. With considerable emphasis they may well assert what I once heard an old Dane declare, "The more I pray, the less I pray; and the less I pray, the more I pray." This was meant to indicate an advanced state of spirituality where all of life now took the place of specific prayers. Such a group would point to works, generous philanthropy, social reforms, or selfless devotion to scientific research, and insist that these are the devotional exercises of the modern Christian and that they are infinitely more acceptable to God than the fat-ram sacrifices of private and public prayer.

Another group of more orthodox Protestants may banish all devotional exercises, all exercises of self-discipline, all confession, all meditation, all mental prayer much as Luther did, regarding them as "filthy rags" in God's sight, and reaffirm that salvation comes not by these means but only by a sheer act of faith. This radical emphasis is continued in Calvin and is almost savagely enunciated in the Barthian Neo-Calvinism of our time. In a private conversation Karl Barth once pictured himself to me as hanging suspended between heaven and hell and utterly powerless by anything he could do to alter his status, utterly dependent upon God's grace. He would have nothing to say of private prayer. To such a consciousness all "religion" as such must go. God is all, man is nothing, and no act of man's may ever dare presume to reach Him. Away with the historical procession of great Christian saints, away with their writings, away with devotional practices! Destroy them all as idols, props, golden calves. God, sinful man, and the redeeming Christ are all.

Both of these positions have in them basic and elemental truths which seem to me unassailable and which I should accept as true. The first insists that devotions must never be substituted for life and would seek to identify religion with the fabric of our daily social life. The second declares that God may draw men to Him and keep them there before they have ever heard of the Bernardian or the Ignatian or the Carmelite or the Salesian or the Sulpician or any other methods of prayer, and that all devotional exercises are secondary to the quickening power of His love. These elemental truths have been underlined in periodic movements within the Christian church since its beginning. But they are half-truths and they will destroy us if taken alone.

WE ARE AS MUCH AUTOMATIC AS INTELLECTUAL

Christian history, however, is quite as decisive in recording the regular gathering of people for exercises that would bring them into a renewal and deepening of their initial commitment: I mean acts of cult worship, acts of confession, acts of monastic retreat; acts of private prayer including meditation and mental prayer; acts of personal discipline such as fasting, pilgrimages, penances; acts of spiritual reading; acts of specific study of religious principles and teachings. And no amount of intellectual argument about science being the asceticism of modern man, or about doctrines of predestinatory grace or mystical invasion have ever driven the apostles of any generation from recognizing many of these practices as of first importance in their lives. These practices do not replace but encourage and quicken good works. They do not hesitate, however, to hold the lantern of interrogation up to the identification of the religious life with programs of social reform and good deeds or with the selflessness of scientific research, and to query how long these activities can be kept creative unless they acknowledge and continually seek personal contact with an eternal point of reference that keeps them in perspective. These practices do not replace grace. They presuppose it at every point. They are only groping responses, answers to grace that would draw all the rest of the life into a continual answer. But for most men and women they are indispensable responses, and if this scaffolding is neglected, the projected building of a Christian life is rarely brought past the aspiration stage.

It has always interested me to note how emphatic Plato is in his insistence that knowledge is power, that *to know is to do*. Yet, I cannot be other than faintly amused at the need which this radical intellectual believer in the allpowerfulness of knowledge seems to feel for a kind of insurance coverage to make sure that his noetic faith will not be disappointed. For in the *Republic* Plato gives no small amount of attention to the use of gymnastics and to other forms of group training in order to build up habits in the young that will take no chances on their *doing* following their *knowing*. Auxiliary disciplines have not been omitted from Plato's curriculum after all.

As for the Christian saints and apostles through the centuries, they have been startlingly clear in rejecting any such mentalist or spiritist hypothesis as that which asserts that we inevitably do what we know. They have explored the inner dimensions of life too deeply for that. They would maintain that knowledge had a place, but that in the religious realm it could never exhaustively precede commitment and therefore that we must consider how that commitment can, be assisted. They have been realists in the inward realm, and they are under no illusions about the part played in our lives by the senses, the imagination, the habit mechanisms so intimately related to the body, as well as by the whole emotional and volitional apparatus. They know that in the Christian life there is no leaving of these mechanisms to care for themselves unless they would court disaster, for it is what you leave out that wrecks you. "We are as much automatic as intellectual," insists Pascal, and he prescribes a set of devotional practices that will incline the whole man to respond to God.

Augustine is concerned to have us use to the full these sensory and imaginative avenues of approach in order to bring us to, or keep us on, the King's highway.

Owing to that very order of our nature whereby we are made mortal and carnal, we handle visible things more easily and more familiarly than things intelligible . . . our familiarity with bodies is so great and our thought has projected itself outwardly with so wonderful a proclivity towards them, that, when it has withdrawn from the uncertainty of bodily things, that it may be fixed with a much more certain and stable cognition on that which is spirit, it flies back to those bodies, and seeks rest in the place whence it has drawn weakness. And to this feebleness we must adapt ourselves; so that if at any time we would endeavor to distinguish more aptly and intimate more readily the inward spiritual things, we must take examples of similitudes from outward things pertaining to the body.[1]

John Henry Newman, with a characteristic exaggeration of his point that sounds almost like a form of religious behaviorism, goes so far as to declare:

Man is *not* a reasoning animal. He is a seeing, feeling, contemplating, acting animal . . . Christianity is a history, supernatural and almost scenic: it tells us what its author is by telling us what he has done . . . Instances, patterns, not logical reasonings, are the living conclusions which alone have a hold over the affections or can conform character.[2]

These practices of self-examination, meditation, mental prayer, swift ejaculation, confession, abstinence, simplicity, spiritual reading, then, are all based upon the nature of the mental and bodily mechanisms and are devices for doing three things: (1) The first object is to keep the vegetative rhythm of the animal and secular life from closing its circuit and absorbing the person so exclusively within its toils as to cut him off from response to a deeper order of which the vegetative cycle is only as aspect. "Woe unto you rich, you comfortable, for you already have your reward." These practices are devices, often violent devices for breaking open this vegetative rhythm in order that a person may know a broader rhythm and may experience the health and holiness of natural functions that come

[1] *De Trin,* XI, 1, 1.
[2] *Tamworth Reading Room,* p. 6.

when the vegetative level is brought into this broader orbit. These practices are devices for cutting off retreats into a premature and temporary animal peace, in order that a man may become open to the only order that will not ultimately frustrate him. (2) The second object of these devices is daily to cut down the tree of self-aggrandizement that grows up in our souls and blots out the sight of other men and of God. (3) The third object is to center the full powers of men—their senses, their habits, their bodies, as well as their minds, upon God and His love that it may speak to their condition. In other words these exercises seek to take men to God—and to leave them there.

THE SPIRITUAL EXERCISES OF IGNATIUS OF LOYOLA

There is a book of spiritual exercises that not many laymen in this generation have ever read through. These exercises were set down by Ignatius of Loyola in the 1530's and revised and printed a decade later. They were built out of exercises which he had used upon himself in his cave retreat in Manresa in Spain. He prepared them in order to stir up and to bring under holy obedience the lives of those men who wanted to come into the devotion of his newly-founded Society of Jesus. They are a set of exercises intended to supply a very complete and detailed outline for a four-week retreat in which a man will give himself up entirely to this experience.

The *Spiritual Exercises* are built upon a deep understanding of the psychological nature of man, with a clearly defined goal as to the type of obedience that Ignatius hoped would be produced. He had been a soldier before a cannonball splintered one of his legs. In the long and painful recovery from this wound he had the leisure to consider his life and its purpose. But in his conversion Ignatius only exchanged one uniform for another, and his *Exercises* bear the print of a military drill manual. Even the type of obedience that they would build is military in its cast. He is concerned to produce a disciplined bodyguard for Jesus. Throughout the exercises there are elements of the most profound insight into the moving of men and women out of lethargy, out of drifting, out of world-centeredness and self-centeredness and into a life of commitment to the person and the spirit of Jesus.

Ignatius would reinstate Jesus on the throne of the heart, and he devotes more than three of the four weeks of meditations to a pictorial identification of the life of the seeker with the actual earthly life of Jesus, beginning with his advent and following through the principal scenes of the mature life, the scenes from the Passion of Jesus, and the different scenes of his reappearance after the resurrection. By the use of meditations involving the powers of sight, audition, sense, smell, and taste, involving memory, understanding, and will, involving every type of fitting posture—kneeling, prostrate, standing, lying, by including repetition, review, and personal assimilation, these five one-hour meditations sprinkled through each day—at midnight, on rising, before or after mass, at vesper hour before supper—over the four-week period were designed to bring the person into contemporaneity with Jesus and into an attachment to him that could never be shaken.

This is done after the first meditations have torn the seeker loose from indifference, forced him to consider the nature of all sin, of his own particular sins, of the de-

structive consequences of sin. (I know of no more graphic
instructions for "seeing with the eye of the imagination
the length and breadth and depth of hell" where you see
the fire and its contents, hear the howling of the damned,
smell the stench, taste the bitter tears of sorrow, and feel
the licking of the flames.) They then bring him to consider the foundation—what he is put here for in life anyway ("the truth that our creation, life estate, are for the
glory and praise of God our Lord and the salvation of
our souls"), to consider to whom he belongs, and to consider what changes in his own life will be necessary if he
comes under holy obedience to this. All of these things
are set forth in great detail with many wise footnotes
that are rich in spiritual wisdom.

The *Spiritual Exercises* are the pattern that has been the
point of departure, often the point of deviation, for all of
the great modern systems of the direction of souls that
have come since Ignatius' time. And, as such, anyone concerned for religious practice should come to know them
intimately. Nor is this judgment annulled by the sharp
criticism that has been directed at Ignatius' excessive use
of sensory images. To this criticism, Ignatius has in effect
answered that, just as we begin with sense experience in
this life and move to spirit, so in meditation, while it
would do well to begin with sense images, it is not intended that we shall remain there. Many are not above
using the porter's ladder in order to climb into the upper
berth in a Pullman car, and yet they mount the ladder
without any intention of spending the night on its rungs.

Now I am concerned that the *Spiritual Exercises* be
written anew in our time. I am concerned that they be
written out of as basic an insight into the sensual and

bodily and psychological mechanisms of man as Ignatius possessed, but that they be devised in order to produce another type of obedience: an obedience which is neither military, as is the Jesuit obedience, nor even feudalistically paternal, as is much of traditional piety generally, but which is a type of obedience that becomes a son, not of a feudal authoritarian Father for all of His love, but of a wise and mature Father, a type of obedience that becomes a human friend of "the friend behind phenomena," or that becomes a group of friends of God who are working together in His service.

TOWARD CREATIVE OBEDIENCE

I have glimpsed the nature of this obedience. I once travelled with two Friends through the Scandinavian countries. We were together for five weeks. We knew each other intimately before we began. Each of us knew that the purpose of our journey was not a matter of private employment but of corporate service in the ministry. No one in the group made decisions by right of even delegated priority, although often we divided tasks in order to execute them. Again and again in meetings we found one of us thrust back and another lifted up in the service. Again and again we found our plans remolded, and as we sat loose, things opened, or if we sat stubbornly tight and refused to yield, the result was not enduring. As we came near the end of our journey, we seemed to wear down individual resistance and to be able increasingly to know each other from within, and we became more and more free with each other. Obedience was there. We lived and travelled and dealt with our work and with each other under obedience.

William Penn once wrote of George Fox:

He was of an innocent life; no busybody, nor self-seeker, neither touchy nor critical . . . so meek, contented, modest, easy, steady, tender, it was a pleasure to be in his company. He exercised no authority but over evil, and that everywhere and in all; but with love, compassion, and long-suffering.[3]

There is the record of the fruit of this kind of obedience in a life. I have seen groups, in which individuals had made bitter accusations against each other, come under that authority, and in the midst of corporate, silent prayer first one and then the other of the assailants would ask pardon, and a creative solution of the dispute would emerge. That is a faint hint of the kind of obedience I would have these spiritual exercises encourage.

My wife and I once visited the little Dutch city of Deventer in Holland, where Gerard Groote lived some 550 years ago and where the Brethren of the Common Life were born. One Sunday afternoon we were walking near a great church that had a high flight of stone steps, perhaps thirty-five or forty of them leading up from the street to the entry way. A child of perhaps three had slowly climbed these steps and was now at the top. His parents were strolling about in the street below. Having reached the top, the child shouted and boasted of his accomplishment and they acknowledged it. Then he called to his father to come and get him. The father beckoned to him to come down. In succession the child shouted, screamed, stamped his little feet and went into a rage. But the father only beckoned to him to come down. Finally, he put down one foot cautiously to the first step, then

[3] Fox, *Journal*, xix-xx, Introduction.

another and another, and slowly and carefully he dismounted the steps. My wife and I watched him anxiously. A fall down those stone steps would have had serious consequences. At last, he reached the bottom safely and ran at top speed to the father and mother, who took him warmly by the hands, and they went off together. The costly act of that father and mother revealed creative love to me and that child learned creative obedience. After that they could go hand in hand together.

It is a costly business to draw forth an appropriate obedience to that kind of creative love, and yet it is to draw men and women to respond obediently to a God who offers that kind of love that I would like to see the *Spiritual Exercises* rewritten in our time. And all that follows here might be considered as *preliminary notes* for such a set of exercises, which I hope some reader, if that is his task, after he, like St. Ignatius, has practiced them on himself, has lived enough, has suffered enough, has yielded enough, and has known the needs of others intimately enough, may set down for our use.

ASCETICISM IN THE NEW SPIRITUAL EXERCISES

I personally have little or nothing to say about the use of ascetic practices—of fasting, of keeping long periods of silence, of the simplifying of life, of celibacy—perhaps because my experience of them is more bookish than real. Yet I would not exclude a serious consideration of them from the new spiritual exercises. For none of the saints have ever gotten on without them. In all asceticism the principle of abstaining from things that are precious and good (from food, from speech, from physical comforts, from marriage) for the sake of accentuating something

more good in itself is a sound principle and is sound practice, so long as it is done voluntarily and joyously and not
grimly, and so long as it can be regarded as a matter of
private vocation and is not universally pressed on others.
Like Berdyaev I feel that "there is nothing more repulsive
than petrified lifeless virtues, or than an ascetic turned
mummy and become an enemy of all human impulses."

The older monastic orders have long ago learned that
a man who is "an enemy of all human impulses" makes
a poor monk. I once asked the prior of a Benedictine
abbey some of the qualities which they looked for in a
man who was being considered as a possible novice.
Among other traits he emphasized that any man who was
a confirmed misogynist, who had a hatred or contempt
for, or a fear of, women or for the married state, was
automatically disqualified. The principle seemed to be
that one must possess and prize what one offers up in the
monastic vows of chastity, if the sacrifice is to be creative.
In the long introduction to his *The Flashing Stream*,
Charles Morgan relates a similar case of a woman whose
loquacity was so great that it became almost unbearable,
even to herself, and so she resolved to enter one of the
strictest of women's contemplative orders where perpetual
silence was kept. On visiting the convent the wise mother
superior promptly sent her away telling her that she must
first learn the preciousness of speech by self-control before she came to offer it as a gift to God. To those whose
special calling draws them to give up these precious and
good things either temporarily or permanently, there has
often come a particular holiness and preciousness about
just these things, which the very abstention from them
for God's sake has seemed to help accentuate

The device of these ascetic practices which often re-open men and women to the presence of God and keep them humbly close to the suffering that is the lot of so considerable a part of the world may be replaced in many by their vocations, where they already share intimately in the daily sufferings of others in their own communities. But we are men and women of short memories, and some daily or periodical ascetic practice may be necessary to break the vegetative cycle and to make us "remember," as Theresa of Avila says, "the guest we have within us."

THE CASE FOR "ISLANDS" OF SILENCE

Next, in this new manual of training for the life of de-votion, there should be a presentation of the necessity for taking time for retirement, for going apart, time to be alone and to enter into directed silence. When Professor Spragg, my teacher of plant breeding at the Michigan Agricultural College, wanted to increase a new strain of Rosen rye which he had gotten from Russia and had then bred until it yielded three times what common rye would yield on the same land, he took it out to several farmers who lived on an isolated little island called Manitou Island in Lake Michigan. There, with no other strain of rye be-ing grown on the island, and with the lake a protection from alien pollen, the new Rosen rye might be grown and the strain kept free from cross-fertilization. In this way Professor Spragg was able to increase the pure Rosen rye until he had enough seed to send out to selected grow-ers throughout the state. By this process of year after year putting uncrossed pure seed into the hands of the rye growers of the state, he almost tripled their rye yield on a given acreage. There is no increasing of the pure seed of the spiritual life that does not call for both initial and frequent returns to an island of silence.

The realization of the necessity of such "islands" is not new. Pythagoras required each applicant to his community of scholars to spend a year in complete silence in order to get back to first principles before he would begin to instruct him in mathematics. Francis de Sales would never think of preaching a course of Lenten Sermons without making a personal retreat of several days into directed silence. Sir Thomas More during the years of his heavy obligations as Lord High Chancellor and King's Counsellor took the Friday of each week for retirement into a little building on his estate in Chelsea, where he devoted himself to prayer and spiritual reading.

The psychological population, which is the number of people we are aware of, is estimated by sociologists to have been increased two hundred times by means of the vast network of communications which the past century has brought. In the urban life of the western world we live in a veritable hail of stimuli that solicit our continual response. The tempo of our lives has increased until we feel continually "driven" by life. Our very architecture shuns privacy. A Swedish architect described to me a new office building in Stockholm where transparent glass brick was used for all office partitions. He went on to tell how one occupant was so unhappy that he painted the inside walls of his glass brick in a desperate attempt to recover at least a skim of privacy. Lewis Mumford in his *Culture of Cities* says of this same architectural tendency in very modern dwelling houses:

In throwing open our buildings to the daylight and the outdoors, we will forget at our peril the coordinate need for quiet, for darkness, for inner privacy, for retreat. The home without such cells is but a barracks, the city that does not possess them is but a camp.

Living as we do in this kind of climate of dispersion, withdrawal, going apart, retirement, and being alone become no longer an option but an imperative to anyone who would enter and grow in the Christian life. George Herbert's counsel must, then, be central:

> "By all means use sometimes to be alone.
> Salute thyself; see what thy soul doth wear.
> Dare to look in thy chest; for 'tis thine own;
> And tumble up and down what thou find'st there.
> Who cannot rest till he good fellows find,
> He breaks up house, turns out of doors his mind."

The new spiritual exercises should, therefore, both counsel the daily withdrawal and give more than vague instructions for the longer periodic times of retreat. This is not the place for such detailed suggestions in regard to the nature of these longer periods of retreat. But a new pattern, including a sustained period of silence which would, however, include spiritual instruction, devotional reading, private and corporate devotions, and manual work something after the fashion of the Iona Community in Scotland, has much to commend it for a fresh approach to this type of exercise. Experiments in this country with precisely this type of exercise have brought great inward refreshment to many of those participating.

This new set of spiritual exercises must not stop, however, at counselling a time of daily or periodic withdrawal. They must also teach an undisciplined mind and will the proper use of such a period. If it is to achieve its deepest goal, it must become more than a period of general relaxation or even of relaxation to the surrounding world of nature. I like to read Thoreau's *Walden Pond* from time to time and I find that it cleanses me from some of the fevers of modern complexity. But it is of little help to me for that deeper fever known as multiplicity of heart. For that disease more penetrating remedies must be sought than those the Cosmic Yankee could provide. Therefore, the exercises should provide for more than relaxation in the presence of nature. They must direct the seeker to meditation and to prayer and they should give specific instruction in each, at the same time that it made clear that the diversity of ways that men approach God or that God approaches men may recast all of these instructions for any given man.

MEDITATION IN THE NEW SPIRITUAL EXERCISES

Meditation should be explained as a voluntary act of the mind, in which the mind out of the infinite subjects for thought at its disposal deliberately chooses to concentrate and continually to re-present to itself for consideration these particular scenes, these particular questions, these particular ideas which are the subjects of its meditation. It resolves to cease to flit over the world at large and to *think of these things*.

Is this not auto-suggestion? Yes, it is precisely that, and we ought to drive away all fear of the nickname which a decade ago so terrified religious people. For what is auto-suggestion anyway? Instead of the mind submitting itself to the objective tyranny of hetero-suggestion, in which the external stimuli determine the content and direction of its thought, in auto-suggestion it exercises a wise asceticism, pulls up the drawbridge, and as far as possible becomes inaccessible to new stimuli or outer suggestions. Then it chooses out of the vast riches available to it one or more specific areas and focuses its attention upon it. The meditator now determines the suggestion that shall be considered. It is auto-determined; it is auto-suggestion. And the fact that auto-suggestion is possible is one of the most remarkable evidences of the freedom of the human mind.

Meditation need not, and should not, enlist only the ideational mind, but should make wide use of the whole sensory imaginative powers. And it is here that these exercises have much to learn from Ignatius of Loyola, who knew, better than we seem to know, the truth of Marcus Aurelius' saying that "our lives are dyed the color of our imaginations." The use of the scenes from the life and death and reappearance of Christ should be central in the new exercises as they were in Loyola's. The value of hanging the picture gallery of the mind with these scenes and of keeping them freshly before us by frequent, prolonged revisitation, as in meditation, can scarcely be exaggerated. The drawing out of the senses in each of these scenes should be encouraged.

Listen to Ignatius' instructions for meditating on the Nativity scene:

It will be here with the sight of the imagination to see the way from Nazareth to Bethlehem, considering length, width, and whether such way be flat or whether through valleys or hills; likewise looking at the place or cave of the Nativity, how large, how tiny, how low, how high and how it was furnished . . . see the persons . . . our Lady, and Joseph, and the handmaid, and the infant Jesus after He was born, making myself a poor bit of a body and an unworthy little servant, looking at them, studying them and serving them in their needs, as if I were there present, with all possible readiness to serve with all possible reverence.[4]

In the next two separate hours of meditation this exercise and a previous one on the Annunciation are repeated, "noting always some more striking portions in which the seeker has felt some enlightenment, consolation or desolation." And in a further hour of meditation the five senses of the imagination are passed over these two objects of meditation, first sight, then hearing, noting the things they say or may say, then smell and taste, and finally "to touch with the touch, as for instance to embrace and kiss the place where such persons tread and sit."[5]

Even in this brief extract from Ignatius on the enlistment of the sensory imagination we are made aware that this is no leisurely promenade through the Louvre. This is an *exercise*. And the seeker is stirred to participate in the action, to help at the birth scene, and in later meditation to join Jesus on his tramps through Palestine, to kneel with the weary disciples at Gethsemane, to bear His cross on his shoulders on the way up to Calvary, to gather in desperation in the throng at the cross and to walk with Him to Emmaus and sit at bread with Him. Beyond this, in each meditation there is the consideration of what this scene means for your life. In the light of it, what must you do to serve him this day? And in the colloquy, or what Francis de Sales calls "the little nosegay," with which each meditation is to end, the seeker is instructed to talk to Christ "just as one friend speaks to another," as one asks oneself, "What have I done for Christ? What am I doing

[4] *Spiritual Exercises,* ed. Rickaby, p. 91.
[5] Ibid., pp. 94-95.

for Christ? What ought I to do for Christ?" And having talked out these questions carry away some specific flower of insight or plan of action from each hour of meditation. These little plans of action may even be written out and returned to again and again through the day in the swift little prayers, the ejaculations, that do so much to restore us to obedience. The *Spiritual Exercises* furnish us with a whole library of such suggestions on the use of sensory imagery in the early stages of meditation.

In a modern set of spiritual exercises, however, there is equally the need for specific meditation on another feature of the Ignatian meditation, namely, upon the end and purpose of life, so that again and again we are brought to re-examine what we are here for and in the light of this to re-evaluate what we are uniquely commissioned to do. "There is no more desolate or Ismaelitish creature in nature than a man who has broken away from his true genius," wrote Nietzsche. "There is no reason to attack such a man, for he is a mere husk without a kernel, a painted cloth, tattered, sagging, a scarecrow, ghost, that can rouse no fear and certainly no pity."[6] This can always best be done in the presence of someone, and once again we see that it is not by accident that Ignatius suggests that when we are beginning to learn to meditate on what we are here for, on the *Foundation*, or on our sins, we do so best by imagining ourselves in the presence of God or in the presence of Christ. Let this examination be made in Their company. Once again the military image of Christ, the Captain, supplied by Ignatius may well be replaced by a Friend or Father with creative love, by a love that draws and burns in the same stroke.

[6] *Thoughts Out of Season*, II.

Of the soul in the presence of Jesus, John Henry New-man writes: "There is a pleading in His pensive eyes—Will pierce thee to the quick and trouble thee." This image of wounded love transforms the Ignatian military figure into a Presence that calls for an obedience that is neither mili-taristic nor feudalistically filial, but is an obedience that binds free men to that which can alone receive their com-plete devotion without exploiting them. It is in this Pres-ence that the meditation should consciously enter.

These meditations should also include a contemplation of sin and of its consequences, and of our own sins. Here again the sense of doing it in the presence of another, of confessing at the foot of the cross, of facing sin in the presence of a departed one is of great assistance, and the sense of wounded love rather than of an oriental poten-tate's wrath or the terrors of a shrieking, stinking, sizzling pit will mark the setting of the modern exercises.

This sense of wounded love, that strikes at the sinful obsession with self, is uppermost in the *Theologia Ger-manica* where its unknown author wrote: "Nothing burn-eth in Hell but self-will." William Law puts it in extreme form when he declares in his *Spirit of Prayer* that "from eternity to eternity no spark of wrath ever was or ever will be in the holy triune of God." George Tyrrell, although he is speaking of preaching, puts the basis of the revision of such a meditation with great precision in a posthu-mously published book of his:

Hence instead of Hell-fire, I should preach the hollowness of the self-life in and out, up and down, till men loathed it and cried 'Quis me liberabit?' And then I should turn men to the Christ-life, not only of Christ, but of all Christ-like men, and make its reality, solidity, eternity stand out stereoscopically.[7]

These modern meditations must not stop with personal sin but must go on to social sin and to its results, to the responsibility we bear for each other, perhaps even to the arousing of the spirit of an Origen who cannot believe that the whole travailing creation will ever stop until every soul has been redeemed, and even to Tyrrell's sense of corporate affection which he expresses in a letter to von Hügel written in 1902:

I don't think you understand how absolutely, and indeed culpably little I ever cared about my own soul, my present and future peace, except as a condition of helpfulness to others. . . . Like Moses, I had rather be damned with the mass of humanity than saved alone or even with the minority.[8]

There must be no saccharine piety about the counsel which these new spiritual exercises give on the use of meditation. "From silly devotions, God, deliver us," pleads Theresa of Avila with her blunt realism. These meditations are work, strenuous, voluntary work, and the learning to concentrate and hold the mind on them is for many far harder than most discursive reading and writing. A sailor boy was once taking an abbreviated Ignatian Meditation and was meditating on the *Foundation* that man is made to praise his Creator and is made for salvation. He was found pacing up and down the room stamping his foot from time to time and saying, "Damn it, it's true; damn it, it's true." I am not suggesting this as a pattern for your meditations, but quite likely education of the will

[7] *Essays on Faith and Immortality*, p. 156.
[8] M. Petre, *Von Hügel and Tyrrell*, pp. 115-116.

was in progress here. Even when undertaken in repose and quiet these meditations are, as has been said earlier, acts of voluntary and directed intensity by which we loosen ourselves from the secular and vegetative and self-absorbed cycle and open the way for another order to enter.

MEDITATION YIELDS TO PRAYER

Helpful as such meditations may be, they are and can never be other than an exercise to open and prepare the person for prayer. And while the new spiritual exercises can never do more than incite to prayer, they must contain a deep enough notion of prayer to make all those who do not practice it have an acute sense of their poverty. Even Ignatius at the close of his manual insists that all the exercises are nothing but preparation for the prayer of affection and should drop away if and when it comes, just as we turn off the lamp when the sun comes up. For while there are elements of conscious guidance in prayer, in its deeper levels it becomes a simple, loving response to the creative love of God, and the pray-er may be taken far beyond where he has guided the prayer when he gives over the reins freely. In the new manual, therefore, all should lead up to prayer where not will or intellect or emotion is central but where the root or ground or principle in a man's nature that is beneath all of these is joyously exposed to this cooperation with God.

Augustine calls this underlying principle "desire," but he does not mean by it an emotional affair.

For thy desire is thy prayer; and if thy desire is without ceasing, thy prayer will also be without ceasing . . . There is interior prayer without ceasing, and this is your desire. What-

ever else you do, if you do but long for that sabbath, you do
not cease to pray. If you would never cease to pray, never
cease to long after it. The continuance of your longing is the
continuance of your prayer. You will be ceasing to speak if
you cease to love. The chilling of charity is the silence of the
heart. If love is without ceasing, you are always lifting up your
voice; if you are ever lifting up your voice, you are ever longing for something; if you are longing, the rest you long for
is in your mind.[9]

This making of prayer as the deep, creative longing of
the ground, Augustine once more expresses in a burst of
aspiration:

My whole heart I lay upon the altar of thy praise, a holo-
caust of praise I offer to Thee. Let the flame of Thy love set
on fire my whole heart; may I wholly burn toward Thee,
wholly on fire towards Thee, wholly love Thee as though set
aflame by Thee.[10]

This emphasis upon prayer being the soul's deepest desire, however, is a linking of the life of the pray-er with
the prayer. It means that the prayer means as much or as
little as the man behind it, and if he remain brittle and
cross and stiff-necked, his prayer will be infected. Martin
Buber in his book of ancient Jewish legends has drawn a
vivid picture of a man who went into a synagogue to pray,
but who found that the synagogue stifled him. From floor
to ceiling it was full of dead prayers, prayers that had been
said by worshippers only with their lips, but that had
behind them no buoyant intent of deep desire to lift them
to God. Inward prayer assumes that the whole man is
behind the prayer and that his life is being ordered in

[9] In Ps. 38:4.
[10] In Ps. 137.

accord with his inward yearning, which the prayer expresses.

Isaac Penington puts it very simply when he says:

By prayer I do not mean any bodily exercise of the outward man; but the going forth of the spirit of life toward the foundation of life for fulness and satisfaction; the natural tendency of the poor, rent, derived spirit towards the foundation of spirits . . . Remember, oh my soul, the quietude of those in whom Christ governs, and in all thy proceedings feel after it.

In Cologne, early in 1940, a much-beloved professor of philosophy, Peter Wust, lay dying after a long illness. His pupils sent in word to him and asked him to give them a parting message of counsel from his deepest experience of life. He sent back to them the following message:

The magic key is not reflection, as you might expect from a philosopher, but it is prayer. Prayer as the most complete act of devotion makes us quiet, makes us objective. A man grows in true humanity in prayer. Prayer is the final humility of the spirit. The greatest things in existence will only be given to those who pray. In suffering one learns to pray best of all.

This "final humility of the spirit," prayer, may be expressed so simply that it would seem almost a violation of its nature to elaborate the aspects of it. The Curé of Ars found one of his peasant parishioners often spending hours kneeling before the altar, utterly motionless, and obviously bent on speaking with God. One day the Curé asked him what he said to God. "Oh," replied the peasant, "He looks at me and I look at Him." That was all there was to it. Francis of Assisi prayed through the night, "My God and my All, what art Thou and what am I."

That utter and complete loving back with the longing and concern to bring every area of your own life, and to bring other persons or institutions or situations that stand outside of creative obedience into an agile response to this source of love is, of course, the heart of prayer. All confession, petition, intercession, waiting prayers and adoration are only aspects of this.

These exercises must give counsel in the use of the prayer of confession where a soul comes under the gaze of God and where in His silent and loving Presence this soul is pierced to the quick and becomes conscious of the things that must be forgiven and put right before it can continue to love One whose care has been so constant. It is one thing to be ordered from the table like a naughty boy to go and wash your hands. George Buttrick once told me of how he had sent his son David away from the table on such an errand one time, and as the boy left the room he said, "I'll go, Dad, but my heart isn't in it." It is another thing, however, to discover your own unclean hands when you sit down with someone for whom you care deeply and whose own cleanness arouses in you the awareness of your deficiency. When a child makes this discovery, quietly excuses itself, retires and returns with clean hands, even a parent forgives the delay and rejoices at the initiative. For he knows this time that the child had his heart in this creative act of obedience. Confession in prayer should be depicted like that in the new spiritual exercises.

The new spiritual exercises would recognize the universal tendency of men to carry their longings and desires into prayer in the form of either conscious or unconscious petition. This is not a thing to be encouraged or discouraged. It is a *given*. What is to be encouraged is that in prayer men should hold these desires sensitively enough and open enough and keep them there long enough to sense their congruity or incongruity with creative obedience to God's love. If this is made clear, then a man in prayer, as in free association, can begin anywhere. What matters is what he comes to. "Did thee yield?" the old Quaker asked. "Was thee faithful?" That is what matters about petitionary prayer.

INTERCESSION IS COOPERATION WITH GOD'S REDEMPTIVE POWER

The new exercises should encourage the all too seldom practice of intercessory prayer, what someone has called "unselfishness in prayer," or "loving your neighbor on your knees." Intercessory prayer may have to be called something else, for it does not mean interceding before a magistrate to ask a special privilege for another. It is rather a cooperating with God's already active redemptive powers to let them work in a given person, institution, or situation. It is a loving fellowship with them in the life of God which undergirds you both. There is no other way that friendship can be brought to its deepest fruit.

In 1901 von Hügel wrote his dear friend, Tyrrell, "I can most truthfully declare that no day passes but you are at least thrice definitely in my prayers; as you are one of the little band scattered throughout space, but united, I feel happily confident, in its struggles, prayers and ideals which ever cheers me on to try and do better, to give more, really all, gratefully, and to accept the *something* that comes of it."

Pastor John Fredric Oberlin in his parsonage at Ban de la Roche, on his knees at a given hour each morning to pray for each separate member of his congregation, and the people hushing each other in the street as they passed his house, knowing the time of day it was and what was going on; a New England pastor that I have corresponded with, dropping in at his church late in the afternoon, and sitting in the pew, now of this family and now of that one, holding them up before God that they might be released to let God work in and through them; the little band of friends who dined with the statesman Wilberforce before he went to Parliament to deliver his great address on the abolition of slavery in the British Empire, questioning whether to go with him to hear the speech in the gallery of the Commons or go home and pray that God might work in that situation, and deciding each to go to his own home and to pray; a Japanese girl praying that God might work in her drunken father and that he might respond with the full life she knew was in him, and the father yielding and becoming a member of the little religious community in which a friend of mine is counsellor —the new spiritual exercises will encourage this kind of prayer of cooperation with God, this prayer in which we have fellowship with others in that which is eternal.

Little need be said of the highest form of intentional, directed prayer, namely, that of adoration, of thankfulness to God. To pause in prayer and to thank Him for Himself, for His being what He is, to tilt the heart upward to the Lover and be glad, this has a natural place in all silent prayer. An old man was asked how he prayed, and he replied that he just sat for half an hour a day in a mood of profound thankfulness to God. His prayer was that, and that was his prayer.

THE PRAYER OF ATTENTIVE OPENNESS

But there is a further aspect of prayer which these devotional exercises must encourage if they are to penetrate beyond the anteroom of prayer. That is the simple prayer of attentive openness. George Fox has expressed it with great simplicity:

Be still and cool in thy own mind and spirit from thy own thoughts, and then thou wilt feel the principle of God, to turn thy mind to the Lord, from whom strength comes, whereby thou mayest receive His strength and power to allay all blusterings, storms and tempests. That is it which works up into patience, into innocency, into soberness, into stillness, into staidness, into quietness, up to God with His power . . . Therefore, be still awhile from thy own thoughts, searching, seeking, desires, and imaginations, and be staid in the principle of God in thee, that it may raise thy mind up to God; . . . and thou wilt find strength from Him, and find Him to be a God at hand, a present help in time of trouble and in need.

I remember a brilliant professor who was expressing his impatience with the use of this attentive openness in the meditation periods we try to cultivate in the planned day of our Quaker work camps. "When I sit down in silence I can only think of ways to mend the cistern, of concrete things, and I have to be thinking of concrete solutions or I can't abide it." In all mature prayer this immensely busy, discursive activity of the mind in our professor friend must be wearied out, must be left behind. "Be still and cool in thy own mind, from thy own thoughts." This mood of prayer is not thinking. It is a pausing from the harnessed activity of thought and in a mood of unhurried calm; it is an opening of the mind in all its oneness to its Source.

Here it is that the refreshment, that the renewal, that the healing may come, and here it is, too, that intimations and concerns may develop that no forced, intense, directed thinking would have aroused. If these specific concerns involve a serious change in life, they require testing by further waiting, by subsequent prayer, and at times by exposing them to others. These spontaneous insights may be of crucial importance to the life of the practicing Christian. Theresa of Avila was about to taper off her activity in the founding of new reformed Carmelite Houses, and in a prayer of waiting it became clear to her that "this is not the time to rest." Dozens of Quaker social enterprises have grown out of such concerns.

But this mood of attentive openness need not always be directed as a specific exercise in prayer. Often it steals on involuntarily from one of the other aspects of prayer. Now and then it comes on so gently that we almost waken, startled to realize that we are no longer praying but are being prayed in, that we are no longer seeking but that we are being found. This is the best of all, and when it occurs, all other aspects of prayer are to be left behind and an inner holiday declared; for this is no longer intentional prayer but communion.

PRAYER AS WORKING COLLECTEDLY

These devotional exercises, however, must not be content to encourage a practice of prayer that is cut off from the rest of life. Professor William Ernest Hocking and Charles Bennett have presented most impressively the conception of alternation, where we work and wear our spirits down and then pray and build them up. Francis de Sales has likewise given us an image of our filling up a vessel full to the brimming in prayer and then trying to carry it so delicately through the day that it shall not be spilled. There is a certain provisional truth about both of these notions. Yet neither of these images exhausts the deepest conception of prayer which these new devotional exercises must encourage. Professor Hocking's notion of alternation, while it expresses a mood we all know too well, still tends to depict prayer and life as too mechanically detached from each other. Francis de Sales' image of the brimming cup is a temporary aspiration, but it is soon discovered as too vulnerable for use in this world. For the world that you and I know is too rough, too unsteady, to keep any such brimming cup from spilling before the first few moments of the day are passed, and if this truly expresses the relation of prayer and life, discouragement is bound to overtake us. We must present a hardier image of the role of prayer in these spiritual exercises.

The new exercises, then, must seek to prepare the life of the pray-er to make it able to live, not simply in the times of prayer, but continually close to the center. "Though my head and my hand be at labor, yet doth my heart dwell in God," says Jacob Boehme. Dom Chapman says of the real goal of prayer:

Remember that the proper result of contemplative prayer is simplicity in the whole life; so that a contemplative is always doing the same thing all day and all night. He is praying, or having breakfast, or talking, or working, or amusing himself; but he is principally conscious that he is *doing God's will*. The different external activities seem to him a sort of varied outcome of one continuous internal intention as if in a long walk: one goes up hill and down, in rain or sun or wind, but the act of walking remains the same all the time, the same movement of the legs, but sometimes easy, sometimes hard, sometimes pleasant, sometimes unpleasant.[11]

Here is practice *in* the presence of God that is beyond feeling and temperament and easy inclination. It makes prayer become less an alternation to ordinary life, less a brimming cup held out above life, than life's constant companion.

Meister Eckhart has put all this with his customary deftness:

One should learn to work with this contemplation in him, with him, and emerging from him, so that one allows his inner life to break into his activity and his activity into his inner life so that one becomes accustomed to *working collectedly*. If they can both happen in him, that is best of all, for then he becomes a fellow workman with God.[12]

This is the goal of these new spiritual exercises and the norm of the devotional life by which they are to be checked. The norm is not whether they make stiff Christian soldiers, or whether they produce feudal Christian liegemen, but whether they draw men and women in the thick of life to live as creative apostles, to *work collectedly* in His service. If they can help accomplish this end, this generation can no longer afford to neglect this fresh concern with Christian nurture. And one of my readers may have laid upon him the concern to refashion Ignatius' service for our time and to give to the western Christian world the sharply realistic devotional manual that it so desperately needs.

[11] *Spiritual Letters,* p. 138.
[12] Pfeiffer, Sect. 50, p. 573.

CHAPTER IV

DEVOTION AND THEOLOGY

I KNOW of no better way to enter upon an examination of the relation between devotion and theology than to recall two scenes, one depicted in a great painting and the other described in a mediaeval legend. If these two images could be constantly recalled, all that follows might quite suitably be considered an elaboration of the theme which they depict.

The first is a painting by Albrecht Dürer, portraying the "Adoration of the Magi." Here the three wise men of the East are gathered reverently about the infant Jesus. After a long and difficult journey wisdom has at last found the object which can call forth its unqualified adoration. And as they kneel and lay before this infant their gifts, it is as if both the life of the wise man and his gifts found themselves searched, humbled, gathered, centered, simplified, and returned to the bearer.

The second image comes from a thirteenth century legend. If you were to choose the two wisest men in Italy of that century, you could scarcely do other than to name the Dominican monk, Thomas Aquinas, whose learning and piety had earned him the title of the "Angel of the Schools," and Bonaventura, the general and the chief intellectual ornament of the Franciscan order. The legend records a visit which Aquinas paid to Bonaventura and a day they spent together in learned conversation. Before leaving, Aquinas asked if he might see Bonaventura's library. Bonaventura took him to his cell, opened the door, and, pointing to the crucifix before which he prayed, said quietly, "There it is."

In these two images of thought where wise men, men who have pressed reason to its very boundaries in order to find what they sought, have felt and followed the necessity of an ever-renewed abandon, an ever-renewed offering up of themselves and of their wisdom to the Source—in these symbols there is contained the germ of all that I have to say about devotion and theology. For I wish to point out first that great theology springs from devotion. This is so obvious that I shall do little more than to state it. Second, and primarily, I want to show that great theology may only be understood through the aid of this background of devotion, and I shall develop this at some length. Third, and finally, I believe it is important to realize that great theology is always subject to revision in the light of the effect which it has upon the devotional life of the millions, and this I shall merely intimate from time to time and leave you to develop if it interests you. From this it will be clear that the emphasis here will be on theology's debt to devotion. But another essay remains to be written which could with considerable cogency develop devotion's debt to theology.

THE REVIVAL OF THEOLOGY IN OUR TIME

We are living in a day when a new hunger for Christian theology is springing up within the free churches of our country. This has come after a considerable period of decline, a period in which theology was held in a position of contempt. The sign that a friend of mine saw in a book store window which read "Second-hand Theology For Sale," represented about the level of esteem in which theology was held by most free church attenders and even by students preparing themselves for the ministry. In its place sociology and economics, comparative religion and, especially the psychology of religion flourished and tended to absorb the place in theological studies which Christian theology had once occupied.

Today the theological seminaries of the free churches are strengthening their courses in systematic theology, student and lay interest is quickening, and even if students do not settle into their theological reading at Phillips Brooks' seminary pace of fourteen hours a day, the Church Fathers are being read again, important theological books are being written and translated, and a genuine revival of interest and concern for Christian theology is under way. The names of Gilson, Barth, Brunner, Berdyaev, Kierkegaard, von Hügel, Maritain and Nygren are becoming well known to ministers and to laymen who read; and the vigor and courage and sweep of their focus upon the central issues of the Christian faith is witness to the fact that although, with one exception, these men are largely the bearers of others' wisdom, yet they mean to make it far more difficult than it has been in the past two decades for Christian laymen and ministers to discuss man's problems from a point of view that was only peripherally, only faintly conscious of man's fundamental kinship to the God of the Christian revelation.

These men have once again revived the genuine task of Christian theology and have seen it to be their work to interpret the relationship of God and man and of the social and physical worlds in the light of the revelation of God's and of man's nature that is to be found in the Hebrew tradition that culminated in Jesus Christ and that has continued in the Christian community which he established. The task of the theologian is, however, always twofold, and these modern interpreters have fully recognized this. On the one hand, the theologian is the custodian of the old, revealed truth, and on the other, he is charged with the ever new task of interpreting this ancient, revealed truth to a world of swiftly-changing interests and ideas.

Theology must keep before its generation the central problems of existence, but it must do more. It must interpret the Christian approach to these central problems of existence in the light of this ancient revelation of the nature of God, of man, and the world, and do it in the most inviting, plausible, persuasive, doubt-dispelling fashion possible. It is for this reason that, while classical systems of theology remain of importance as landmarks and as architectural designs that show that it can be done, theology must yet be rethought and rewritten in every generation, if its real task is to be performed.

But in between this ancient, revealed truth and the intensely modern world of swiftly-changing concerns and emphases, the theologian himself is placed, and if he is to accomplish a really great work, he must be more than a disembodied mind. The greatest theologians have been men for whom that ancient, revealed truth has come alive and has seized them with a sense of its commanding significance for the life of their generation. At times it has come alive in an individual and personal way through a striking experience of conversion; at times it has come alive through the intensity of devotion of a corporate community and its practices, of which they were a part; and at times it has come alive through the embodiment of that devotion in the life of a saint who has deeply impressed them. But unless this ancient, revealed truth has come alive for the theologian, unless he is contemporary with it, his theology is likely to be colorless, without spirit and of little lasting value. And the stream in which the ancient, revealed truth has come alive for him is also likely to do much to give the tone and the accent to his entire position. In other words, theology, while it is wrought out by the mind and best wrought out by an able mind, is, and must ever be, more than a sheer intellectual exercise.

Now not only is the task of theology a double one, but there are also two principal groups for whom theologians write. In the first group there is the unbeliever who must be dealt with, and the plausibility of the Christian revelation must be laid before him in terms which interpret his own experiences better than interpretation which he has previously accepted. Second, and of equal or greater importance, theology has a mission to the believer. For it is one thing to take out a title to new land, and it is another thing to clear it up and make it able to be farmed. There is the stubborn, inward resistance of the believer's pride that keeps ever throwing up new scrub growths of disbelief. There is the tough underbrush of unchanged habit life. There is the prolific relentless questioning of the believer's own mind that seeks to relate his inward core of faith to the secular world in which he lives, a world where the secular sciences are inclined to interpret spiritual values in such a parsimonious way as to rule out what is central to his inward experience. And there is the tendency to interpret the whole of the Christian revelation exclusively in terms of details of the believer's own particular inward experience. Theology must help him not only to clear and dress and plant this ground, but also to keep it fertile and productive and free from extravagant growth.

Now some of us may be contemptuous of theology, saying that the saint is the best theologian, and insisting that the life, the devotion, and the experience take precedence over it. We may be scornful of the way it has fulfilled its task in the past and inclined to jeer at it as the valley of dry bones. But let none of us think that we can get along without some structure in our religious experience. Charles Bennett once recorded a personal experience which occurred while he was riding on a train between New Haven and Boston. As he looked out of the window, he thought he saw on a great signboard, "Gorton's God, No Bones." On closer inspection it turned out, as you know, to be "Gorton's Cod," but this amusing psychological illusion is too perilously close to being an accurate description of the amorphous, jelly-like character of the free church's beliefs about God in the past generation to be really funny.

This structure in our religious beliefs is called for because we have minds as well as emotions and wills. Our truth-seeking minds demand insistently that in matters which are to affect our whole style of life, the wall of separation must go down and we must interpret what we love in the light of the rest of our experience.

The persons or groups who have claimed that they needed no theology have almost invariably been themselves the victims of an unrecognized, implicit theology whose tyranny was evident to all except those under its spell, and which, since it is never subject to examination and review, is forever cut off from the possibility of improvement. Beyond this personal concern it is imperative to realize that we live in a day when Christianity is being attacked squarely and openly by social and racial religions that are appallingly explicit in their own ideology.

GREAT THEOLOGY IS ROOTED IN A DEVOTIONAL SITUATION

Now, after noting in free church circles this revival of a sense of need for theology, and after this brief reference to the important function which it is theology's task to perform, it is necessary to add a strong footnote of caution in regard to the enduring significance of this renewed concern for theology. My own estimate is that this present revival of interest will be of brief duration and will be little more than a cry of desperation that will not create a fresh theology but will only point nostalgically to the theologies of the past, if it is not rooted in the recovery in our generation of the life of devotion out of which all great theology has sprung and must ever spring. And I regret to say that among the free churches I find no corresponding groundswell of devotional renewal in prayer, in devotional literature, or in other practices that reveal devotion out of which this theological rebirth could take both its accent and its direction.

In speaking of these practices of devotion, however, I do not wish to focus upon mere externals, but to regard them as symptoms of that spirit of devotion which no one has ever described more tellingly than Francis de Sales when he declares:

Devotion is simply the promptitude, fervour, affection and agility which we have in the service of God, and there is a difference between a good man and a devout man; for he is a good man who obeys the commands of God although it be without great promptitude or fervour, but he is devout who not only observes them but does so promptly, willingly, and with a good heart.

Unless the devotional life, the commitment to God, and the loving intensification of the life's prompt and swift and joyous response to God are quickened within the free churches, I believe that any revival of theology that may spring indigenously from them is doomed in advance to be a wooden, abstract, and lifeless affair which will soon wither away. For truly great Christian theology, while it is only one manifestation of devotion and is never to be confused with devotion as such, has always sprung from a watershed of devotion, whether it came from Tertullian or Origen or Augustine or Aquinas or Bonaventura or Martin Luther or Jonathan Edwards or John Henry Newman or Friedrich von Hügel. It has not been stimulated, conceived, or written out of the dispassionate deliberateness of an individual or a group deciding that the time had now come when it would be a good thing to write a theology. Nor has the need of the situation alone produced it. It has rather been pulled out of men who had lived in groups, who had felt and known the quickening and renewal of devotion, and who were, therefore, ready and even driven to speak of the need. But if this devotional situation, as manifested by the devotional literature, the saints, and the religious practices of the community, exercises a determinative influence upon the production of great theology, is it not reasonable that in order to understand such a system of theology we should have to be exposed to the devotional situation from which it sprang?

DEVOTIONAL LITERATURE AND THE UNDERSTANDING OF GREAT THEOLOGY

This becomes especially apparent if we consider the nature of devotional literature, which is often the most accessible form of exposure to the devotional situation of the period of some great system of theology. There is something uniquely revealing of the condition of the writer in genuine devotional literature. It is usually strongly autobiographical and yet contains little of the diffuse material that marks most autobiographies. On the other hand, devotional writings are not so subject to the temptations of eloquence as are sermons. Abbé Bremond has written of all devotional literature in a specific reference to Francis de Sales:

Every line written by Francis de Sales or the other great spiritual masters is involuntarily a confidence, a spontaneous witness. One cannot say as much for the majority of sermons. Devotional literature is never Platonic, it addresses itself to the imagination and the intellect solely to influence the will. A devotional book in the inner history of the Christian community starts a vibration.

If we would know the theology of the period, we must know the real bent of the devotional literature that is the source of such a vibration of which the very theology may also be a part.

When, as occasionally happens, the theologian himself is the author of devotional writings, then all that has been noted is especially true. In the four years of his most intense literary production from 1842 to 1846, Søren Kierkegaard, the Danish religious thinker, developed a noteworthy rhythm of writing his books. Along with his weighty aesthetico-theological treatises he wrote and often published on the same day or in the same month little volumes of devotional addresses that revealed the temper of the source-waters out of which the theological writings had come. To understand Søren Kierkegaard's theological writings a reader must above all read them against the background of these devotional addresses which "litmus" the true color of the solution in which this man's life and thought stood.

Not all religious thinkers, however, have produced devotional writings which give so direct a clue as those of Søren Kierkegaard. In some cases the devotional classic has been written by some close contemporary, or the devotional situation has revealed itself not in a devotional book at all but in some saint or some liturgy or some fresh pattern of charity. Yet, it has been my experience in reading the theology of the great men of the past, that it is almost indispensable to a real understanding of their theology that one have the help of a magnifying glass which is supplied by a knowledge of the devotional life out of which this theology arose.

It is neither an accident nor an attempt at diversion but rather a recognition of a deep pedagogical law that, at St. John's College under the Great Books program, when they assign the reading of world classics to students for their weekly tutorials, they pair off a philosophical reading with the reading of a poet or a dramatist. Hence a selection from Plato's *Republic* finds a play of Aeschylus its companion; and a chapter of Aristotle's *Nicoma-chean Ethics*, a play of Euripides; or a series of proposi-tions from Thomas Aquinas' *Summa*, a group of cantos from Dante's *Divine Comedy*. These inward counterparts to the philosophical or theological systems help to illumi-nate the whole and make the philosophy come alive.

Professor Singer, of the University of Pennsylvania, suggested one time that the only way that he could get much out of Hegel's *Phenomenology of Spirit* was to read it like a symphony score, to imagine it set to music, and to get the great sweep of it. What was Hegel's theme song; what was he trying to say; what is it in Hegel that pro-duces those many variations? If it is pedantically puzzled out word by word and note by note, Professor Singer con-fessed that the *Phenomenology of Spirit* had little or no meaning for him. I have since read and reread the *Phenomenology of Spirit* and have found this whimsical prescription of the greatest value.

Jacques Chevalier makes an additional suggestion that seems relevant here, when he writes in his striking book on Henri Bergson:

Now that which truly matters in a man's work, gives it meaning, is its life, and that part of it which will endure is not so much what he said as *what he meant to say*. But to get in touch with that, you must know the man.[1]

Once when I was working on John Henry Newman's *Grammar of Assent*, Professor Whitehead gave me an in-teresting piece of advice that might well take its place with these other two suggestions. He said, "When you read Newman, try always to find out not what he says, primarily,

[1] P. 38.

but what he takes for granted, what he finds it unnecessary to say. Then you will be more likely really to understand him."

Now in reading theology I feel that this counsel is, if anything, still more relevant than in philosophy. For only as I know the man who wrote the theology, as I know the devotional stream in which his life stands, as I know the saints and the religious practices of the period, may I grasp the theme, the unspoken background that makes the theological system live. These factors are like a delicate reagent which scholars apply to old manuscripts in order to bring out the faded ink and make it stand in clear relief again.

THEOLOGY AND DEVOTION IN AUGUSTINE

I have been reading recently a number of Augustine's theological writings especially the treatises written in connection with the Pelagian controversies. I have immersed myself in his account of the nature of man and the nature of man's freedom. Augustine's account of man is familiar to you. Created out of nothing, with the potentiality of an angel but with the *libertas minor*, the "little freedom," the freedom to sin, man out of pride, not lust, chose to defy God, to reject the possibility of the *libertas major*, the "great freedom," the freedom always to choose the good, and chose to set up an inward pattern of defiant pride against God in which you and I, his descendants, share. Tainted with this defiant pride, we cannot, by any efforts we may make, escape from its toils. By all standards of divine justice this defiant pride deserves eternal punishment. Yet, in spite of this desert, God in His mercy and grace has chosen to issue to some whom he has selected a release from this slavery of the defiant will into the freedom of wholehearted loving response to Him. This, in a word, is Augustine's system of Christian anthropology set forth by a great theologian for all men to read. But I confess that I could make but little out of this whole emphasis upon God's creation of man out of nothing, out of man's complete bent to nothingness and hence to impotence within the toils of this defiant pride, or out of the accompanying doctrine of predestination to salvation that excludes all but a chosen group from participating in salvation and, in effect, predestines all but this favored few to be damned.

It is only as I sought to find out what Augustine was really trying to say, what he meant to say, what his implicit inner theme really was, that I could see in these fierce discourses anything other than the outcropping of a mood of theological sadism. This insight into his real meaning did not come, however, until I read the treatises through the glass of the *Confessions*. In this perspective the treatises ring true. They reveal a continuation of the same effort of a proud soul, long sick, long "intent on learning and restless to dispute," long hard and unresponsive to the Divine Flame, "unwarmed by the heat of Thy spirit," finally yielding to God's love and being so overwhelmed with the sweetness that it found itself only able to respond adequately by making of God, all, and by making of itself, of man, nothing. As a hymn of love, as a prayer of thanksgiving "laid at the feet of the rich man who fed him," I can understand how he flung himself at God's feet and laid all of his and mankind's creation to God, and nothing to the material of which he or other men were made, since, for God, the Loved One, all is possible. I can understand how man's vileness in resisting God's patient love can be charged to an hereditary pride, a bent to nonbeing, worthy only of scorn and contempt, and hence that in sackcloth and ashes man can be made into dust, into nothing. I can even understand how predestinationism in this mood is an effort to carry still further the lover's attributing all, utterly all, even the very turning toward God, to the act of the Loved One, thereby excluding all who were not so moved by the Loved One's initiative. The Gospel of St. John says, "Without me, ye can do nothing," and through the glass of the *Confessions*, I realize that Augustine has known and proclaimed this fact.

With the help of the *Confessions* these treatises of Augustine's become the most important of commentaries to help me understand the grace of God, to distinguish between the monkey way of clinging to the mother and the cat way of being held and carried firmly by the mother, a symbol of man's relationship to God. They enable me to distinguish grace from love, where the object is believed to deserve the love and is expected to love back, to recognize that God's grace is lavished upon man without any possible assurance that he will return it, that it is poured out of the largess of God without any connection whatever with the merit or desert of the recipient, that it was lavished at creation, lavished in the gift of Jesus Christ, and is lavished now in the creative act of redemption. Holding the treatises and the *Confessions* together, I come to see afresh what Jesus was trying to teach by his going beyond legal desert or even moral desert and teaching the grace of God in the difficult parable of the payment made to the eleventh-hour laborers in the vineyard, in the parable of the loving father's treatment of the wayward son, in the story of Jesus' ready understanding of the woman's act when she anointed him with precious ointment, or in his final words of forgiveness on the cross. Augustine's almost grotesque emphasis in these treatises upon our debt to God's outpouring of grace, I now see, is not unlike an El Greco painting that distorts in order to reveal. The fruits of this emphasis appear when Augustine appeals to the faithful who have felt God quicken them to let Him have His way in the simplest things, to love back in *all that they do*. Thus we hear Him explaining Psalm 34 to his parishioners in the diocese of Hippo:

If you are singing a hymn, you are praising God . . . Then the hymn comes to an end and it is time for a meal; if you keep yourself from over-eating, you will be praising God. Are you a rural labourer? Then be sure that there are no weeds left in the ground you are digging, and once again this will be an occasion of praising God. Thus by the innocency of your works you will be praising God all the day long.

THEOLOGY BEFORE THE BAR OF THE DEVOTION OF THE MILLIONS

At the same time that the *Confessions* have helped me to receive from the treatises this rich teaching on *grace*, I cannot keep from considering the third point of our inquiry: how, if it is taken literally, does this teaching on the nature of man which Augustine expounded in the anti-Pelagian treatises affect the devotion of the millions. How does this disparagement of man, this confronting him with his vileness, with the hopelessness of his choice to follow God if he be not elected and his virtual predestination to damnation if he be not chosen—how does this affect the religious life of mankind? For while theology is not a mere pragmatic hypothesis, yet, it, too, may deserve Christ's curse that it were better that a millstone be hung round its neck than that it should cause one of his little ones to stumble.

One might even go so far as to say that *any* theology may be questioned if it, when preached from, paralyzes religious life and growth and action. One of the striking things about much of the Barthian revival in Germany was that it was a theologian's theology. While it quickened a number of ministers by convicting them of the shallowness of their faith, when it was preached unequivocally to congregations, it tended to make private prayer unreal, it cut the nerve of Christian ethical discernment by its thundering about the sin-blighted relativity of all man's corporate and private acts, and it set God so far away that He was virtually inaccessible to daily life. There is in the devotion of the millions a bar of judgment for theology that has been too little examined or taken into account.

George Tyrrell in the first volume of the *Faith of the Millions* puts this insight very bluntly.

Rational theology is in some sense an attempt to look at things in a nonhuman, nonnatural way; and it is justified in this endeavor only so far as it tends to cure us of our terrestrial "provincialism"; but it is not surprising that to us things so viewed should seem distorted and unreal, the moment we forget that its use is mainly corrective—that it is medicine and not food . . . Any rational explanation that would make prayer nonsensical, or would encourage laxity . . . create an impression fatal to the sense of liberty and responsibility . . . or would make havoc of the ordinary sane and sensible religious notions of the faithful, is, *eo ipso*, condemned as not squaring with the facts.

When I look at this feature in Augustine's doctrine of predestination, I find the literal reading of the treatises equally impossible without the perspective of the *Confessions*. With the *Confessions* and their exposition of Augustine's own experience of attributing all to God and nothing to himself, the doctrine of predestination is seen to be a projection of this experience, and I am not surprised when I discover later on that Augustine himself shrinks from presenting this withering doctrine of predestination to the faithful. In a significant section entitled *When the Truth Must Be Spoken, When Kept Back* he counsels preachers that it is not always necessary to preach this doctrine of predestination itself lest men be discouraged. The wise Church, charged with the nurture of the devotional life of its millions, quietly allowed this extravagent predestinarianism to lapse into oblivion; and on at least two occasions when it became an issue, with Gottschalk in the ninth century, and with Jansen in the seventeenth, she condemned it in favor of the deeper insight into the grace of God that was the distinctive theological contribution of Augustine. From such an illustration much light is shed upon the wisdom of subjecting theology to the test not only of internal consistency and plausibility but also of its effects upon the spirits of those exposed to its teaching.

Now, once again, I may confront Augustine's account of original sin, of man's depravity, of a bent toward defiance of God that taints and damns each infant born into the world, and I may find in it a relic of an ancient curse from which we have been mercifully redeemed. I may feel toward such doctrine something of the contempt expressed by the Presbyterian clergyman in the meeting of the general assembly in which infant damnation had finally, after years of debate, been voted out of the articles of doctrine, when he rose to his feet and solemnly moved to make the action retroactive. Yet, in the light of the *Confessions* I may see a great insight emerging even here. For the *Confessions* are not at bottom the record of a man redeemed from physical vice, although that is present too. What Augustine did in living with a common-law wife for some fifteen years and substituting another woman for her when she left was common practice, and he was no better or no worse than his contemporaries. The real record of the *Confessions* is of the power of God to bring a brilliant, cultured, proud mind under His yoke, to turn a genius into an *apostle* who has come under Holy Obedience, who has known how the love of God can melt down the hard, stubborn core of a brilliant self-sufficiency and create a sense of new, relaxed pliability. That *pride* is the greatest sin, is written across the pages of the *Confession*, and they become the record of God's conquest of pride, of what the grace of God has done to the proud mind of the Professor of Rhetoric of Milan.

In the light of this I begin to see what is meant by this hereditary defiance of God called "original sin," which is so prominent in the treatises of Augustine. I begin to see that he is only writing a commentary upon Jesus' holding up as the objects of his most bitter invective not the sins of the body but the sins of pride, of selfishness, of hardness of heart, of self-righteousness. And in this emphasis of Jesus and of Augustine there seems to be a major cleavage with Greek thought as expressed in such a mind as Plato. For in Plato there is no talk of a sin of the mind, such as pride, that may keep man from blessedness. For

Plato, mind does not block or blind itself. It is matter that blocks mind. It is the prison-house of the body that keeps the mind in darkness. It is the unruly steeds of the body and its lustful appetites that are opposed to the charioteer of the mind. It is the biological that retards the psychological, and if the mind could dominate all, if by proper education the psychological could assume supremacy over the biological, for Plato all would be well.

In Augustine the enmity to God is no longer charged to matter or body versus mind, or to the biological versus the psychological. The reluctance to yield to God is laid to pride and is thus placed within the mind itself. By placing the whole struggle within the mind or the will of man Augustine has placed it in that very part of man for which he, as a man, is uniquely responsible, and hence man is made to bear the full brunt of the responsibility for his defiance of God. Now it is proud, self-centered mind against the mind of Christ in us. It is autonomous, self-sufficient mind, against a thankful, responsive God-centered mind. And the whole tussle is depicted as a psychological struggle between the hard, proud bent to self-sufficiency and autonomy on the part of the restless, active mind, and the willingness of one who becomes a loving, tender, humble agent of God to yield to the Christ-mind. It is the split mind versus the whole mind.

This whole contrast is enhanced still more by Augustine's account of God's grace, of His love, of His tender concern. Against the Great Lover man's hardness of mind and heart becomes still more despicable. Under Jesus' and Augustine's analysis there is less opportunity for evasion than under the Greek. I have had too little of Plato's education; therefore I am not to blame. In my body the biological horses were by heredity too strong for the psychological charioteer to manage; therefore I am not to blame. No, says Augustine, *you* on whom responsibility rests have not learned because you did not *want* to learn, and you must never seek to evade by ignorance the distinction between ignorance and unwillingness to learn. You sought proudly to protect your own integrity against the grace of God, you have tried to save your life and to resist abandonment to God's grace, and by so doing you have lost it. Apart from this grace of God you are isolated and cut off from both life and truth.

Now in Augustine the return of the mind to its Source becomes an affair of all or none. It is not a matter of a little more education or of a little more evolution from the biological up into the psychological plane or of a little more charioteer skill. These are all movements in the same proud direction. They are still on the broad way that leadeth to pride and destruction. There must be a change of direction, a volte-face, a loss of life, an act of submission, of yielding, of assent, on the part of the proud mind to the Divine love. There must be a discovery on the part of that proud strain of mind that only in its death, its crucifixion, can the true life of the mind be known, a life of the mind that finds itself planted in the Divine love "that burneth and never consumeth." Out of this union of the loving mind with God, real insight may come, "for Truth," says Augustine, "unveils itself to him who lives well, prays well, and studies well."

Thus illuminated by devotion, out of which these insights sprang, illuminated by Augustine's own experience as set forth in the *Confessions*, and checked by the devotional response that it has aroused from strong proud minds as diverse as Luther, Pascal, and Papini, who look to Augustine as their liberator, and by millions of less prominent folk who have known pride for what it is by Augustine's help, the account of original sin as set forth in Augustine's treatises becomes for me an intelligible and stirring contribution to the psychology of the soul. Yet apart from the *Confessions*, it remains a pre-Christian legalistic formula, a forbidding and vicious dogma.

THEOLOGY AND DEVOTION IN BERNARD OF CLAIRVAUX

Once again, in Bernard of Clairvaux I can read the mystical theological treatises on *The Love of God* and find described there the four stages of love: (1) love of ourselves, (2) love of God in order to get something for ourselves, (3) love of God for Himself, and (4) love of ourselves only through our love for God. I find the last stages of this very difficult to fathom until I come upon a sermon to his monks in the *Canticle of Canticles*, where Bernard shares the devotional experience out of which this theological insight has come:

But now bear with my foolishness for a little. I wish to tell you, as I have promised, how such events have taken place in me. It is indeed a matter of no importance. But I put myself forward only that I may be of service to you, and if you derive any benefit, I am consoled for my egotism; if not, I shall have displayed my foolishness. I confess, then, though I say it in my foolishness, that the Word has visited me, and even very often. But although He has frequently entered into my soul, I have never at any time been sensible of the precise moment of His coming. I have felt that He was present; I remember that He has been with me; I have sometimes been able even

to have a presentiment that He would come; but never to feel
His coming or His departure. For whence He came to enter
my soul, or whither He went on quitting it, by what means
He has made entrance or departure, I confess that I know not,
even to this day. . . .

You will ask, then, how, since the ways of His access are
thus incapable of being traced, I could know that He was
present. But He is living and full of energy, and as soon as
He entered into me, He has quickened my sleeping soul, has
aroused and softened and goaded my heart, which was in a
state of torpor and hard as a stone. He has begun to pluck up
and destroy, to plant and to build, to water the dry places, to
illuminate the gloomy spots, to throw open those which were
shut close, to inflame with warmth those which were cold, as
also to straighten its crooked paths and make its rough places
smooth, so that my soul might bless the Lord and all that is
within me praise His Holy Name. Thus, then, the Bridegroom-
Word, though He has several times entered into me, has never
made His coming apparent to my sight, hearing, or touch. It
was not by His motions that He was recognized by me, nor
could I tell by any of my senses that He had penetrated to
the depths of my being. It was, as I have already said, only
by the movement of my heart that I was enabled to recognize
His presence and to know the might of His power by the
sudden departure of vices and the strong restraint put upon
all carnal affections. From the discovery and conviction of my
secret faults I have had good reason to admire the depths of
His wisdom; His goodness and kindness have become known
in the amendment, whatever it may amount to, of my life;
while in the reformation and renewal of the spirit of my mind,
that is, of my inward man, I have perceived in some degree the
loveliness of His beauty, and have been filled with amazement
at the multitude of His greatness, as I meditated upon all
these things.[2]

[2] Condensed from Sermon 74.

Here is the source of that apex, of that ladder of love that illumines the whole of the mystic way, that makes the mystic's goal of the beatific fervour, which always crown his theological system, intelligible. Here is the reality, of which the system is a symbol; and the gap between the second and third stages, between the love of God for what He gives, and the love of God for Himself, is seen to be so great that only one who had known the third would ever dare place them in a series. In mystical theology, as in dogmatic theology, devotion alone lights up theology and makes it able to speak to us.

When I read in the *Summa Theologica* of Thomas Aquinas, I find there his differentiation between the cardinal and the theological virtues, between the cardinal virtues of justice, temperance, courage, and wisdom, which spring out of and order our natural relations with each other, and the theological virtues of faith, hope and charity, which according to Aquinas are only given to us from above. The artificiality of the division is as repulsive to me as it has always been to critical ethicists. Yet, when I read Thomas Aquinas' commentary on the Divine Names, when I read his hymns on Corpus Christi, when I know that as a devout Dominican monk he was a regular participant in the Roman Catholic mass where in the sacrament he is given that which he does not deserve and can never merit, I begin to understand. When I have no reason to doubt the experience attributed to him at the close of his life in which his chronicler reports that after certain inward experiences he lay down his pen, saying, "I have seen too much; I can write no more," I begin to come into possession of what Thomas Aquinas is trying to show, namely, that above the natural Greek and Stoic virtues there is a range of virtues that is shared only as a gift, a range of virtues that come upon us, to use a favorite figure of von Hügel's, more like receiving a golden shower from above than like a coral reef that is built up from below. And instead of repulsion I begin to wish that he had gone on and shown us how, when drawn upwards from above by these theological virtues of faith, hope and love, the very cardinal virtues of justice, courage, temperance and wisdom are transformed. For there is natural justice, natural courage, natural temperance, and natural wisdom, and there is also each of those same qualities raised above itself, as we sense from time to time.

BONAVENTURA: THE INFLUENCE OF A SAINT ON A SYSTEM OF THEOLOGY

It seems to me that it is a stroke of greatness in Étienne Gilson when, as an interpreter of medieval theological thought, he has devoted almost one-sixth of his book on Bonaventura's theology to an account of the life of the Franciscan general, Bonaventura, and to his relation to his master, Francis of Assisi. For once more, this great theological system of Bonaventura's, like the foreshadowing of Renaissance art in Giotto, or like the wave of practical philanthropy that swept Europe through the Third Order of the Franciscans, sprang out of the devotion of the single-minded Francis of Assisi, for whom all books but one were superfluous. And to neglect the life of such a saint or the devotion it released is to stand helpless before the thought-children and, in particular, before Bonaventura, the theological thought-child which Francis bore.

What can Bonaventura mean by insisting that the end of man is the communion with God in the ecstasy of beatific fervor? What can he mean by insisting that when a pagan philosopher and a Christian confront the same proof for God, they are not subject to the same laws of convincement? What does he mean by insisting that only as body and mind are purified and made ready by ascetic discipline, a discipline which burns in its truth by freely-chosen renunciation of things good in themselves, can they receive truth? What does he mean by humility as the principal virtue that lays the axe at the root of concupiscence? We can never know what he means until we recognize him as a son of Francis of Assisi and remember that the culminating experience of Francis' life was his experience of communion with the crucified Lord at La Verna. He means, as Francis revealed and taught, that not he that says he will follow but he that quietly takes up his cross, begins repairing the church, if that is his task, and follows Christ, may know the truth of the existence and nature of the Christian God, the passionate loving Father of all, the God who is concerned less for intellectual admirers than for disciples.

This, Francis had clearly brought out for Bonaventura by his own singleness of life. While his fellows prayed, "Oh Lord, help us to do thy will, to a certain extent," Francis prayed to God as his All. Bonaventura saw that Francis was no religious record-breaker, but simply one who loved Christ so completely that he could not bear his own life and went about mending it as best he knew how. He saw that Francis took this way of life before he had any assurance of what lay ahead for him, or that others would join him; he learned as he went, and knowledge unfolded with increasing abandonment to God. Bonaventura also saw the boldness of Francis that revealed the aspect of faith which is fearlessness toward the full consequences of the act, a fearlessness that may release the vision from the astigmatism caused by the eye of the soul continually readjusting itself in trying to focus simultaneously on all of the obstacles to the act of commitment or of charity.

In the second place, it means that he has not missed the ascetic note in Francis' life that made him free to love the natural world as no minnesinger or troubadour ever loved it, because he loved the natural world in that which was beyond it, its Source. It means that if you want to understand Bonaventuran humility, you must know intimately the *Little Flowers of St. Francis* and recall such an incident as the one where Francis and two companions are on their way up to La Verna. Francis is so ailing and so weak that he can walk no further, and one of the companions went in to beg the use of an ass from a peasant who agrees to accompany them a short distance. They helped Francis to mount the animal, and as the peasant trudged along, he said, "If you see that brother Francis of yours, tell him that I hope he is as good as men say he is." Whereupon Francis, ill as he was, slipped off the ass's back and kissed the peasant's feet. In this incident or the famous chapter, *What Is Perfect Joy*, Francis reveals how humility and a very hunger to identify oneself with the suffering Christ can transform the most extreme suffering into joy when it is suffered for Christ. Such are the setting and background to Bonaventura's philosophical interpretation of suffering and humility, and without them or some inward baptism in them Bonaventura's theology remains an almost insoluble enigma.

IN CONCLUSION

I would bring this discussion of the relation of devotion and theology to a close by reiterating that not only in the thirteenth century with the theology of Bonaventura but in any century we must know the saints, the devotional literature, and the religious practices, if we would really grasp theology's meaning. You will find Nicholas of Cusa's little devotional gem, *The Vision of God*, invaluable in unravelling the mystical theology of his *De Docta Ignorantia*. You will find a helpful key to understanding the theological position of the younger Luther by reading his favorite devotional manual, the *Theologia Germanica*. You can scarcely expect to comprehend seventeenth-century Anglican theology if you do not know Lancelot Andrewes' *Private Devotions*, or to fathom Jonathan Edwards if you do not know John Bunyan's *Grace Abounding*. Robert Barclay's *Apology*, the only really formidable piece of theology the Quakers ever produced, must be read along with George Fox's *Journal* and Isaac Penington's *Letters*, the record of these two early Quaker mystics, if the deeper import of the *Apology* is to be grasped. Nor will you see the real bent of Newman's thought in his theological treatises unless you know intimately his early *Plain and Parochial Sermons*, which are nearer to being an inner revelation than even his polemical *Apologia*. To understand von Hügel's massive theology no small assistance is given if you know his devotional master, Abbé Huvelin, or his adored saint, Catherine of Genoa.

Here in the life of devotion and in its records is to be found, unless I am mistaken, the source-mother of theology, the glass through which theology is to be read, and a healthy proving ground for bringing to light the theologians' extravagances. Dürer's three wise men would seem to have confirmed our impression of their wisdom by lingering before the crib, and the free church theologians of our time might well be drawn to serve an ample apprenticeship in Bonaventura's library.

CHAPTER V

DEATH'S ILLUMINATION OF LIFE

~~~~~~

WALT WHITMAN was attending a funeral one day. Just ahead of him a girl of fourteen was standing before the open casket as though she were transfixed. Walt Whitman put his arm on her shoulder and spoke to her. "You don't understand that, do you?" he asked gently. And as she dully answered, "No," Whitman added, "Neither do I," and they moved on together.

Before another's death and its meaning the fellowship of the living, when they are honest, cannot do other than confess to each other their bewilderment. Running through all the emotions of irreparable loss, of loneliness, of fear, of relief, of outraged resentment, or of resignation, there is and there must be this common note of mystery, "I do not understand."

All of the theological and philosophical arguments begin and end before this curtain of mystery. They pretend to banish the curtain by declaring that it is not there, or with a great and laborious intellectual display of effort they lift it, and we hear the convincing creak of the machinery as it rises. There can be no doubt of it; this thinker has really raised the curtain. But on closer inspection we find that when confronted with death our eager expectancy toward this argument undid us, for this curtain which our thinker raised was only the outer curtain, and behind it hangs a curtain that may bear a less forbidding emblem but yet is quite as effective in hiding the stage. Behind curtain after curtain, there is always another.

I have no hope of raising the curtain that will make us able to understand the death of another. That must always be curtained with mystery. When Jesus heard of Lazarus' death, he wept. When Mary Magdalene thought of Jesus in the tomb, she was consumed with grief and mourning. Weeping and mourning are appropriate responses to the passage of another beyond the curtain. They mark a kind of frustration, a wearying-out of the surface-mind's feverish desire to understand and classify and order this event in the smoothly handleable, frictionless, exhaustively communicable categories of the mind. The prostration of grief, the weeping and mourning point me beyond this conventional effort of the classifying mind to the more costing way in which to draw near to the one thing needful in the matter of the death of another. They point me to the more costly business of examining the meaning of my own approaching death.

For the death of another can shock and stun and sadden me. But it cannot reach me with its meaning and its illumination until I have taken it into myself and examined it in the light of my own self confronted by death. In the self, my self, I have a nub that I believe I may know both from within and from without. Here in my self is a nub that, confronted by its own death, is threatened with extinction not only in the outer evidences that it can collect about itself, in its outward estimate that it is continually revising about itself; but here before death, the evaluator, the estimator, the very impartial spectator itself, which knows itself from within, is also threatened with extinction. Now, death is no longer any statistically inevitable affair. Now, death becomes a direct threat to that *Me* which does the choosing, the deciding, the committing, the yielding, the caring.

Death illuminates life. Before the prospect of its own death this *Me* finds itself dynamically searched. (1) It finds itself groping to see if it has found a ground or a medium that gives some evidence that it will carry the *Me* in this moment of extremity. What have been its past experiences of being sustained through the drastic change that assaulted and threatened to consume the *Me*? (2) How has this *Me* been assisted in a grasp of the ground and core of its nature by the situations that have not only threatened to consume, but to individuate it, situations like the prospect of my own death, that have demanded an unequivocal choice from it, situations that have planted themselves on my threshold and refused to be dismissed by the appearance of a butler, uniformed in a conventional response, but that have kept rapping insistently at that door for the master himself to appear? (3) In the course of these encounters with life, has the *Me* known what it is, not alone to be sustained through change and to answer in person the summons to individuation? Has it also known a qualitative drawing that satisfies its deepest yearning, that raises up that which is good in it and yet at the same stroke inflicts the pain of pains, as it strikes at sin in the life? (4) And finally by confronting my personal death and discovering the ground and meaning of true self-abandonment, am I brought to discern the difference between much of the contemporary manic flight into acts of service, and what appears to be the recklessly careless unconcern for life or death of those mature ones who, having faced and known the meaning of death, then reveal a broad freedom to pour themselves out in redemptive acts for others? What, then, is death's illumination of life in these four areas?

If a consideration of the meaning of its own personal death can wring answers to these questions from its experience, the *Me* will confront death not with an answer, for that would lift the curtain, but with what is still more important—a faith and a faith-born courage in the final leap as well as a heightening of each hour and day of the life that precedes it.

Although every form of plant and animal life is characterized by an implicit resistance to extinction which is usually called a motive of self-preservation, yet man seems to be unique in his capacity to know in advance and to be able to confront the prospect of his own death. If this capacity to contemplate his own death is unique in man, however, it is a quality which gives him great pain to exercise and which provokes in him strong resistances against using it. In his *Two Sources of Morality and Religion* Bergson goes so far in his discussion of the biological ground for the low, static type of religious practices as to suggest that these practices are virtually biological devices for suppressing the fears which a frank facing of an individual's own approaching death may be expected to arouse in him.

Because of this power of resistance, anything short of a major emergency seems unable to drive a man into taking consideration. In the recent treatments of schizophrenia, a shock treatment has been devised so that by the use of insulin or metrazol or, still more recently, by a violent elec-

trical charge applied to the head, the system of the schizo-
phrenic patient appears to be so alarmed and threatened
that, in order to throw off this sudden threat of dissolution, it shocks the mind out of its absorption in phantasy,
and the patient is thrust out into the world of reality again.

It may be one of the tasks of philosophy as well as of a
high and dynamic type of religion to compel individuals
to contemplate not the death of another but of themselves,
so that in the course of this attack upon the very citadel
of the self, evidences may be erupted and a contact with
reality established that no milder treatment could arouse.

MODERN WESTERN SOCIETY'S CONCEALMENT OF DEATH

If the degree of resistance produced by the contemplation
of my own death should be regarded as an index of the in-
security of the individual or the society, our own generation would have to be declared peculiarly fearsome to the
considerations involved. For we live in an aspirin age, when
any discussion of death is regarded as morbid, as defeatist,
as a betrayal of, or a treason against, life. The mortician
carefully deletes the word death from any notice which he
may send. In fact, he has created a fashionable business
out of making death as much like life as possible, and the
families of the deceased pay handsomely to be deceived.
The stark realities of death and of the dissolution of the
body are all hidden from us by modern embalming, by
elaborate bed caskets, and the other accessories of the profession.

The late Richard Cabot, who proposed throughout his
career both as physician and as Professor of Clinical
Medicine at the Harvard Medical School that doctors
should tell their patients if there was a reasonable pros-

pect of death, so that they might prepare themselves for this great adventure, found himself jeered at by most of the medical profession as a fanatic. In their minds it was the physician's duty to reassure the patient that he would, of course, live, even when he knew and when the patient strongly suspected that death was imminent. In this practice there is no denying that the doctor may have followed the surface wishes of his patients, for enough patients have changed physicians in order to get a still more optimistic report of their condition, to give a doctor some ground for insisting upon his privilege of indulging himself in medical mendacity in such situations.

The matter does not stop at professional practice, however, for a sufferer's own friends and especially his family enter wholeheartedly into this game of deceit. It is as though they were facing a common enemy which they dare not acknowledge to their own consciousness; hence, they unite in assuring the invalid that he is looking much better, that he will soon be well, and that they will in no time be busy again in active life together. If a friend called and dared to talk with the invalid about death and its meaning, it would be considered hopelessly bad form and might result in the family denying him access to the sick man again.

Gone from this modern period is the stern realism of the day when the pew in which the worshipper sat during the service was only a few rods from where he knew his own body would in a few swift years become one with the earth again.

An aged Norwegian peasant who in the fall, before the roads become unpassable, has his son purchase and bring home a wooden coffin in case he may need it that winter, and who keeps this chest in the parlor and visits it at times, would in our world be considered a melancholic horror. Yet the peasant could scarcely understand, or, if he could, he could scarcely exaggerate his contempt for the softness of the society that deals in such elaborate concealment.

This unwillingness of modern western society to face the prospect of approaching death appears again in its glorification of youth, of that period when the surplus of animal vitality is so great that the effusion screens off any hint of the significance or meaning of a life that is grounded in another source of vitality. The cult of staying young, of keeping the youthful figure, the youthful skin pigmentation, the youthful hair color, the youthful zest for being continually immersed in a hail of external stimuli is slavishly worshipped.

The world of men is made to exist essentially for the youthfully mature specimens of the genius. The restriction of human values is limited to a single age out of the seven, and this is made the whole focus of life. Human beings are infants, children, youths, only as preparation for this early and brief maturity, and the fading end of life has value only in proportion as it is able to cling self-deceivingly to the illusion of the continuance of the years of buxom fullness.[1]

For such a civilization devoted to the cult of the body and its world, old age and death are nothing short of a calamity and, of course, must be concealed.

The swollen pride with which such a generation views its technical discoveries that have annihilated distance and brought disease under control and, by means of social collectivism, have gone far towards annihilating poverty may also be a factor in this concealment of death. For,

[1] Hartley Burr Alexander, *God and Man's Destiny*, p. 17.

finally, before the door of my own approaching death, technical discoveries, medicine, and social collectivism seem strangely outside and irrelevant. Another medicine is called for, and none of these can procure it.

In its thinking the modern civilized mind feels thwarted by the decisiveness and finality of the prospect of its own death. For the modern mind has banished these factors in its habits of thought in favor of the more tentative and relative. The clean-cut divisiveness of Heaven and Hell have been smiled away; right and wrong have been softened into relatives. Surely there must be some way that this menace of my own approaching death can be handled that can modify its apparently definitive decisiveness. And the modern mind has decreed that there is.

By this general conspiracy of concealment in regard to death, by exalting youth's nuptial zenith, by a continual glorification of the achievements of the collective, by the aid of medical sedatives and opiates upon the occasions of decline, by humanistic references to a vicarious social immortality, by impressive sociological pronouncements that one generation moves on, only to make room for ever new and more creative forms, the decisiveness of my own death is almost blacked out, and the aperture of the awareness of my transformation at death is almost squeezed shut.

But in a man, even a modern man, who retains his sanity, the blackout of the decisiveness of his own personal death, the closing of the aperture of his awareness of his own death, is seldom complete. What a ghastly horror if a man were able to live so like a beast that he was utterly dumb to his own approaching death and barred from more than a sensitivity to the appetites of the moment! Yet we need have little fear of such a prospect. For there come moments by day and hours by night where nearly every man and woman who lives has asked in his heart of hearts what his own death signifies, what, if anything, comes next. "Is there?"; "Is there not?" "If there is, then —what?" "There comes a midnight hour," says Søren Kierkegaard, "when all men must unmask." This means when *each* man must unmask, and "each man" means that there are no exceptions.

It becomes necessary, then, to see what the prospect of unmasking in my personal death means to me, and hence to look at death with steady eyes. Instead of sedatives we might rather ask that our minds be dipped in acid that they may be eaten clean of fear and staleness and made rawly sensitive to death and the light which death casts upon life. In this we may be willing to lay aside the fashion of our time and be more open to listen to ages that found it good to consider the approach of death and who found that death illuminated the nature and the meaning of life with a clarity that no other consideration could approach.

DEATH'S THREAT STRIPS THE ME

First of all, what is this death which I confront, and what will it do to me? My own death means a major crisis, a major change, a major transformation. There are religious apologists who try to derive some comfort by attempting to lessen the character of this change, and they quote with avidity the scientist's report that the very cells of our body are continually changing and that my body is in a constant state of death and renewal. Death, then, becomes only a continuation of what is already at work. At first sight this may seem impressive. But a more careful examination of the scientific account of the death of the bodily organism distinguishes clearly the hiatus between death and this bodily renewal in life. Science defines death as "an irreversible cessation of the interchange of living substances." There is a finality about that account of death which as far as this body is concerned, crumbles any previous promise which this observation may have brought. No, death means that I must go through the needle's eye, and that most, if not all, of what I have come to identify as my permanent possessions will be stripped from me.

In so far as the medium of my body is concerned, my family will be taken away, my vocational position will in a few short weeks or months be given to another, my dreams and plans for the things I would accomplish for my fellows must now be relinquished to others, my possessions must go: my house will be sold or rented or passed into the hands of others, any income that I may have will go to others, my books will distribute themselves into the libraries of others. Yet, even all of this could happen as it has happened, in some cases even more than once, to many European refugees, and still the crisis might stop short of being the crisis of death. I must give up what Francis of Assisi called Brother Ass. I must be stripped of my body. This may be a painful operation not only in the physical pangs of death but because all of these other possessions of mine clutch the body tightly as their one hope of preservation.

The contemplation of this prospect searches a man dynamically to see whether he has found any power in him or about him that can bear him through such drastic change which none but the ignorant or the cowardly will ever seek to minimize.

John Donne in a famous sermon on *The Gate of Death* speaks tenderly of that hour when

. . . the sun is setting to thee and that forever; thy houses and furnitures, thy gardens and orchard, thy titles and offices, thy wife and children are departing from thee, and that forever; a cloud of faintness is come over thine eyes, and a cloud of sorrow over all theirs; when his hand that loves thee best hangs trembling over thee to close thine eyes.[2]

A generation ago the Spanish thinker Unamuno, in his *Tragic Sense of Life,* directed each of his readers to ponder the event of his own death.

Although this meditation upon mortality may soon induce in us a sense of anguish, it fortifies us in the end. Retire, reader, into yourself and imagine a slow dissolution of yourself—the light dimming about you, all things becoming dumb and soundless, enveloping you in silence, the objects that you handle crumbling away between your hands, the ground slipping from under your feet, your very memory vanishing as if in a swoon, everything melting away from you into nothingness and you yourself also melting away, the very consciousness of nothingness, merely as the phantom harbourage of a shadow, not even remaining to you.[3]

Before such a meditation a man is laid bare. In confronting such a change all the customary supports have been withdrawn. He has become vulnerable, infinitely vulnerable:

[2] *Sermons*, ed. L. P. Smith, p. 196.
[3] *Tragic Sense of Life*, p. 42.

Naked I wait Thy love's uplifted stroke!
My harness piece by piece Thou hast hewn from me,
And smitten me to my knee;
I am defenceless utterly.

Rainer Maria Rilke murmurs, "I am afraid, I am filled with a nameless fear at this change." Now there is no turning around on this road and slipping off up some side street. For death is a one-way master road in which there are no exits. In such a moment a man is searched as under a terrible crystal in order to find in what he has put his trust. In the face of such a change, do I know, have I been quickened by, have I lived from anything within myself that is not of dust or of earth or of flesh or of time? Do I know any knot in the thread of my life that will hold when I am pulled through this dark cloth of death?

This moment of anguish neither can shape nor desires to shape out refined philosophical distinctions. Yet, it is capable of arousing an elemental "No, that is not it, that will not bear me now," as I confront the complex empirical *Who's Who* self that the world has known me by. And this moment is capable of eliciting a whispered "Yes, I believe that is it; I will risk my weight on that," when it feels the stab of that *Me* out of which the choices come, the yielding, the commitment, the letting go and the holding on. I may quiver as I acknowledge that this living *Me* has for so long allowed itself to become identified with the *Who's Who* self that the pain of detaching it now is almost unbearable, or, as I admit in a flash of insight, that in order to protect myself from the pain of certain costly decisions, this *Me* had long before put its hand to the ghastly terms of neurosis and accepted a slave status. Yet, in this moment of trial, I can only acknowledge this *Me* that consented to sinning, this *Me* that yielded itself in acts of love, this *Me* that in a few brief moments may have felt its outer defenses shattered and its inmost core shot through with "bright shoots of everlastingness," and in acknowledging it, realize that this inner *Me*, and it alone, is the frail vessel in which I must face this storm of transformation.

DEATH INDIVIDUATES

We have until now been considering the illumination of the life of this inner *Me* in which the threat of the drastic change of death was central. Yet, not only is the *Me* threatened with this searching change, but in death it must face that change alone. In death the way becomes narrow and the gate strait. If throughout its life the *Me* has depended upon companionship, advice, the group, the crowd, and a middle way in their company, in death, at least, it is faced with what it means to be an individual, to look upon itself as an individual and to assume responsibility for itself as an individual. For over this frontier the path contracts and all must travel Indian file. Death is an intensely individual affair. Death isolates, and before the prospect of death all props are withdrawn, all leaves are cancelled, all makeup is removed, and a man's individual being is brought into view.

Søren Kierkegaard's *Purity of Heart* is haunted by an image of man alone before his creator. From some references in his *Journal* I suspect that Kierkegaard imagined the situation of death to be something like the exposure of a man on his beloved Jutland heath on which the sparsity of all vegetation left no place where one could run or dodge or crouch or lie prone and not still be exposed to an observer's view. In the words of the Negro spiritual, "there'll be no hidin' place up there." He describes this singling out process which death involves, the process of isolation that dissolves away the crowd, that shuts out the many voices that have enabled him to wheedle and compare, and that leaves his own conscience alone before the Eternal.

In eternity conscience is the only voice that is heard. It must be heard by the individual. It must be heard. There is no place to flee from it. For in the infinite there is no place; the individual is himself the place. It must be heard. In vain the individual looks for the crowd. Alas, it is as if there were a world between him and the nearest individual, whose conscience is also speaking to him about what he as an individual has spoken, and done, and thought of good and of evil . . . Eternity never counts. In eternity you will look in vain for the crowd. You will listen in vain to see whether you cannot hear where the noise and gathering is, so that you may run to it. In eternity you too will be forsaken by the crowd. For in eternity crowds simply do not exist . . . Yes, here in the temporal order it is possible that no individual can ever succeed in dispersing the crowd . . . the crowd shouts mockingly at God, "Yes, now see whether you can get hold of us"; yet, since it is difficult in the rush of the crowd to distinguish the individual, the sober countenance of eternity quietly waits . . . Eternity scatters the crowd by giving each an infinite weight, by making him heavy—as an individual.[4]

In the prospect of death a spiritual gravitation is revealed. Each is indeed made heavy as an individual. Lines here and there from Psalm 139 might furnish a kind of refrain to Kierkegaard's severe text:

[4] *Purity of Heart*, English translation, pp. 170-177.

Thou hast searched me and known me . . . Whither shall I
go from thy spirit or whither shall I flee from thy presence
. . . The darkness and the light are both alike to thee . . .
Search me, oh God, and know my heart, Try me and know
my thoughts.

Now at the prospect of death evasion of responsibility
for myself as an individual is over. Three modern writers
have cast this scene. A. H. Clough in his *Dipsychus* has
chosen to have even the tempter turn on the waverer at
the close of his life:

Heartily, you will not take to anything.
Whatever happen, don't I still see you living no life at all?
Will you go on thus until death end you? If indeed it does.
For what it does none knows. Yet as for you,
You hardly have the courage to die outright.
You'll somehow halve even it.

Ibsen, in spite of his questionable thesis of conditional
immortality, has in his *Peer Gynt* shown the individuating
power of the prospect of death. Peer Gynt, the genial
trimmer, who in the spring sends out a shipload of idols
for the China trade and in the fall helps finance a troop
of Christian missionaries China-bound, the man who has
always hugged the middle course and comforted himself
by comparisons with others in his generation, Peer Gynt is
met on a narrow path by the Button-molder, God's emis-
sary, who has arrived to collect his soul and to take it to
be melted up again. For in an entire lifetime Peer has
failed to imprint any distinctive stamp upon it. Peer bargains and begs for a few more days or hours in order to do
something from out of the very core of his *Me*, but is refused. Bitterly he cries out, "This Gynt cessation, this

casting-ladle business, it filleth my inmost soul with re-
volt." But the Button-molder is firm, "Thou hast set at
nought thy life's design. Into the pot with other spoilt
goods."

Charles Vildrac in his poem *The Farewell* has written
of a man left swimming in the sea when a great liner
went down. "He acknowledged his appointed end" but he
wished

> To use for slow and holy profit
> The last warmth of his body,
> The last illumination of his mind . . .
> There was at the heart of this man
> A life unknown to himself,
> A life simple and still full
> Of childlike faith.

As his life and its meaning came clear to him,

> Water burned in his eyes
> But it was not the water of the sea.

At the poignant prospect of my own death life is often
clarified. The *Me* learns what it is to be an individual:
what it is to drift and what it is to steer a course; what
it is to be an interchangeable cipher of the world, and
what it is to have taken on a number from within; what
it is to have surrendered to surface determination, and
what it is to have responded to a call from another quarter.

In the aloneness, the isolation, the singling out, the individuating process of death, there is an emergence of
what it means to be the responsible bearer of a life design. And with my life thrown into such perspective by
this confronting of my own death, I am shaken out of the
lethargy of procrastination and of my well-established

habit of moving to lay all difficult decisions upon the table and brought to see the earnestness and the urgency of assuming responsibility for my life. I come to see that now indeed is the eleventh hour, that now is eternity.

This clarification seems to be little aided by formal religious and philosophical guarantees of the imperishability of the self as I face this consuming change. Any such evidences seem a bogus passport that only a naïve traveller would presume to present at this boundary line. Now the only evidences that matter seem to be dynamic or functional. Before death the questions that the *Me* is faced with are less ontological than existential questions.

Does the *Me* know what it is to lose itself, to be given away, consumed, used up, and what does such an experience reveal to it about itself? Is the *Me* a good jumper, is it a good self-spender; in short, has it learned to die in life? Has it leapt in life and reached the other side? Has it been sustained as it passed over a cleft that gave none of the usual guarantees about the nature of the landing place on the other side? Has it spent itself on the highest thing it knew without assurances of compensation? And, as it gave all it possessed and was worn out in the service of its cause, as its own claims on life were worn away and it felt its own powerlessness, did it discover what it was not to live, but to be lived? Did it come upon some invisible means of support which released it to go on with ever greater abandon?

Or the questions may be reversed and the issue remains the same. Has the *Me* learned that in attempting to make itself invulnerable, in shielding, in defending, in hoarding itself, it has voided its life design? Has it discovered by the painful stagnation of such self-preservative tendencies that *it was lent to be spent*? Has it ever sailed the tight wooden ship of its pretensions to invulnerability close enough to the magic mountain of some abandoned life or power that was itself highly vulnerable and found to its consternation, that the magnetic power of this mountain had drawn out all the nails and left of its ship only a pile of floating planks? When this happened, has it abandoned the wreck and made for the mountain with a good heart?

These are the dynamic questions with which the *Me* is confronted at the prospect of death. And before this prospect the memories that sustain and that illuminate life are memories that do not fear but welcome these interrogations.

PRACTICE IN DYING: THE LITTLE DEATHS

These memories of the times when we took what John Donne calls the "Northerne Passage," when we risked, when we practiced dying by dying the little deaths, only to have something come alive in us, are not conclusive evidence of immortality. They are at best only hints and intimations, but they seem to have prepared us for change and individuation, and so at death they are good company.

How good to remember, now, that time in life when as a parent we saw a child off to school that first morning, to feel the wrench of his departure, to know that now he must make his own way, be taught by others than ourselves, risk life by accidents and suffer in countless ways from which we can no longer shield him! We trusted him to life that morning, and as he disappeared from sight, we died a little death. But in that death something still stronger inside us seemed to emerge and he was more our own because we had let him go.

How good to remember the first day we gave a daughter in marriage to a young man who was not bone of our bone and who could scarcely be expected to understand and to treat this precious daughter as we knew so well to do at home! How great the risks and uncertainties of love and marriage! How important this girl's future was to our heart! And then the scene cleared, and we gave her away to this young man. And we died another little death, only to feel a new dimension of caring for these two rise up in us and the meaning of an old Sanscrit proverb come clear: "That which is not given away is lost."

How good in this hour to remember the day when our mother or our father died! It seemed as if they must always be there, that they must always come to us in illness or distress, that they could always be relied upon. Any tasks well done, there was a secret sense of their approval; any recognition our work received, it was the prospect of their satisfaction in that acknowledgment that made up the greater share of any worth that it possessed. Then perhaps the mother died, and there came a rush of mingled loss and of being cut adrift. Now you were alone at sea. Now you must steer your course alone. Now you were adult. Now you bore the full responsibility.

Rainer Maria Rilke describes in the *Journal of My Other Self* how the physician fulfilled his father's wish at death and pierced the father's heart. At that moment the aloneness seemed complete, and he spoke to himself, "Today, Brigge and nevermore." He describes the walk which he took on that day about the town of his boyhood. Now it seemed a town for grown-up people. On this day the child in him had died the little death. But the *Me* in him knew a new depth to its love for and relationship with the father and yet this *Me* knew its own root as never before.

How good to remember the time that I knew that I should die if I owned to another my guilt in some affair, and how I owned it and died, only to discover that what had died in me in that miniature death was my egotistical pride and that beneath the death of humiliation there is still the true *Me* that lives and breathes more freely for this loosening of its bonds!

How good to remember those sleepless nights when I feared to relax to sleep lest I should meet there what I was afraid of, and lest I should not be able to stand the encounter; and to remember how I slowly discovered that to die the little death of sleep meant trusting the goodness and the forgiving character of the conserver of the *Me*, and how I learned to let go to the source of life as the earth lets go to the spring and how I was carried away and refreshed and strengthened and restored!

How good to remember that illness in which, my body stale, torpid, dull and apathetic to my demands upon it, I practiced dying, I practiced wearing my body like a loose garment! There I discovered that instead of quenching the *Me*, the utter weakness of my body seemed to intensify the *Me's* claims to possess a life of its own.

How good to remember how I have let go what went before and have faced and welcomed each age of my life as it came, and in mature age how I have discovered that the dying back of my body has given me more occasion to be at home, and to keep my own heart warm by living in it! Until that time I had never fully grasped what that seventeenth-century writer had meant when he suggested that it was a wonderful thing to recognize the advanced age of a person less by the infirmity of his body, than by the maturity of his soul.

And, finally, how good to remember how in prayer one day my stiff, tight, detailed petitions were all blown aside as though they were dandelion fluff, how I stopped praying and began to be prayed in, of how I died and was literally melted down by the love of a Power that coursed through my heart sweeping away the hard claimful core, and poured through me a torrent of infinite tenderness and caring! Blind with tears, I suddenly knew and felt the very being of suffering people whom I had recently visited, gathered, and loved in the very heart of God, who drew me to care for them as I had never done in my days among them. Theresa of Avila once wrote of this death in prayer: "Nothing seemed to satisfy my desires; every moment my heart was ready to burst. It seemed to me as if my soul was being torn from me. It was a kind of death so delightful that my soul would gladly have prolonged it forever."

The remembrance of these exercises in dying the little deaths helps to make us able to inhabit a *Me* whose nature it seems to be to die into life, to discover an invisible means of support as it is loosened from its tightly clutched settings which masquerade as life.

Rabindranath Tagore has given a discerning description of this loosening process:

There are men whose idea of life is static, who long for its continuation after death only because of their wish for permanence and not perfection; they love to imagine that the things to which they are accustomed will persist forever. They completely identify themselves in their minds with their fixed surroundings and with whatever they have gathered, and to have to leave these is death for them. They forget that the true meaning of living is outliving; it is ever growing out of itself. The fruit clings to its stem, its skin clings to the pulp and the pulp to the seed, so long as the fruit is immature, so long as it is not ready for its course of further life. Its outer covering and its inner core are not yet differentiated, and it only proves its life by its strength of tenacity. But when the seed is ripe its hold upon its surroundings is loosened, its pulp attains fragrance, sweetness, and detachment and is dedicated to all who need it. Birds peck at it and it is not hurt; the storm plucks it and flings it to the dust and it is not destroyed. It proves its immortality by its renunciation.

PRACTICE IN DYING: LIFE IN EXTREMIS

But such renunciation, such detachment, such limberness, such abandonment to the ripening processes of life and of death on the part of the *Me* as Tagore describes make a severe strain upon even our store of remembrances of the little deaths in order to yield to it. Faced with death some seem to require for their help the recalling of instances of an even deeper shattering of the hull than these highly natural occurrences of miniature deaths that have been described here. There are some who can only practice dying, who can only grasp the power of the *Me* to assimilate death and emerge from it, as they are confronted with major crises and see every shred of security removed.

The act of Cortez in burning his own ships in the Mexican harbor, ships that represented the last possibility of retreat, of return to Spain in the event of defeat, is a symbol of what some need to have before them at death in order to understand this limberness of the *Me*. For now

the mutinous band of Cortez' companions had nothing
to do but to advance, nothing to do but to let go to the
new. Anything short of such a crisis may leave an easier
way out, and that for them is an evidence that stops short
of illuminating the way the *Me* reacts to death.

In his beautiful account of flying, called *Wind, Sand
and Stars*, the French aviator Antoine de St. Exupéry tells
of a test flight over Libya where he and his companion
crashed in an uncharted part of the desert. Their food
reserves and water were destroyed in the crash except for
a few oranges. The first two days were spent close to the
plane in the hope of rescue. Then they each planned ex-
ploratory walks that would take them half a day's journey
away from the wreck of the plane, and they would spend
the other half day in returning to meet at night. Finally,
after several such tours, with the oranges gone and themselves well spent, they realized that now there was only
one hope: to abandon the plane, their single tie with
civilization, and to set out at dawn, now not on a half-
day tour, but to go until they found hospitality or perished.
That night they burned what remained of the gasoline
over the wreckage of the plane in a last desperate hope of
being sighted, and at dawn they left this one remaining
shred of security and set out. Now all returning was
stripped from them. They were alone in the desert, but for
meeting a friendly Bedouin on the second day when they
had all but given up hope, we should not have had the
story.

In facing any crisis short of my own death, there may
still be something that I cling to, some landmark, some
crumpled wreck that I may hope to repair, some rescue
by others. But when base is abandoned for good, then the

Me knows whether it is open to invisible support. Then it has direct access to what it means to lose all. Then it has a dynamic firsthand account of whether what is called *all* in this loss was really all, or whether the dark passage through this foreboding womb was but a birth.

No one has described this death and birth more simply and directly than Haniel Long in his *Interlinear to Cabeza de Vaca*, where Cabeza de Vaca is writing to the Spanish king an account of his sufferings in Florida after the decimation of the glittering Spanish military expedition in which he had come:

While we were the subjects of your majesty, we had everything life offers, and now we had *nothing*. To understand what it means to have nothing one must have nothing. No clothing against the weather might appear the worst. But for us poor skeletons who survived it, it was not. The worst lay in parting little by little with the thoughts that clothe the soul of a European, and most of all with the idea that a man attains through dirk and dagger and serving in your Majesty's guard. We had to surrender such fantasies till our inward nakedness was the nakedness of an unborn babe, starting life anew in a womb of sensations which in themselves can mysteriously nourish. Several years went by before I could relax in that living plexus for which even now I have no name; but only when at last I relaxed, could I see the possibilities of a life in which to be deprived of Europe was not to be deprived of too much.[5]

Here is the record of major stripping, a record of death in which the *Me* of Cabeza discovers that it is not dependent upon either the clothing, or the food, or the houses, or the churches, or even the culture of its empirical self but that

[5] Pp. 14-15.

the *Me* is bottomed in a sustaining life that prior to this act of painful birth it did not know.

Yet, for many "to know what it is to have nothing, it is necessary to have nothing." So long as some can touch bottom, they will never trust the water and learn what it is to swim. When Søren Kierkegaard sought to explain what was meant by true abandonment of the *Me* to the Eternal, he chose the case of an incurable sufferer. He understood the need of doing more than reminding his readers of the little deaths, of the suffering involved in a temporary illness. Even reminding them of the condition of a sufferer in a critical illness, where there was still a faint chance of recovery, was not enough. For in each of these cases some prospect of the return to the old securities was still present, and so long as this return door is still ajar, total abandonment may not be at hand. Only in the case of an incurable sufferer, one who could never be well again, one for whom the door back was forever closed, one who could not touch foot on the bottom of customary life expectations, only by placing such a sufferer in their midst, did Kierkegaard believe that he could expose his readers to the true nature of abandonment, where the *Me* can die to every conventional support and yet can by yielding come alive to its invisible bastions as never before.

DEATH AND AWARENESS

These remembrances of the little deaths and of the more violent dyings, which in the mature individual have made the inner *Me* emerge as the conventional securities receded and have given to men the only satisfying intimations that the great adventure of my personal death is but a greater step in its direction, have not stopped at this alone.

These remembrances have given firsthand evidence no only of the *Me* being sustained and conserved through the changes and of the isolating aloneness of death. They have quite as convincingly witnessed to the *Me's* growing awareness of being searched, qualitatively searched in this change; and in this searching they have become aware both of their own grossness, and of their longing to respond to this qualitative source that confronts the *Me*. It is as though in each change, each isolation, another hull had been removed and the *Me* became more and more vulnerable not alone to being changed again, but to the meaning of the change and to the only thing that seemed to matter through all change.

A parent who releases a child into life not only discovers that they can both live when separated. But the parent is thrust through by a shaft of love for that child and a sense of what that child's life means, at the very moment when there is revealed to himself a sense of his own possessiveness and of his own dullness and of his own cruelty with a poignancy that he never knew as long as he clutched the child to himself. Now it is as though the altitude had suddenly shifted and the atmosphere were thinner and the ultraviolet rays of love could burn themselves into him as they had never done on the lower level.

An adult who loses a mother in death not only discovers that he must now live from a deeper root of self-responsibility after this change, but he is usually swept by a feeling of caring for her that makes him in one swift glance both thankful for what she has done and meant to him in a way that he has never been before, and at the same instant conscious that he is searched to the very core of him for his own failures to make a full response to that love.

One who in prayer has ever been prayed in and has felt the defenses go down and the coursing of love pour into his life knows well the qualitative searching that accompanies this sense of being sustained. This *Other* that one confronts in the moments of the little death, as the *Other* that one faces at the moment of the great change, seems to draw us to itself and yet by its very tenderness to judge down and make us aware of that in us which must go before we can bear to be in its presence.

This experience may be thrown into still sharper relief for me if I will admit the evidence of those persons often called saints whose lives have been lived so intensely that they may serve me as a lens to magnify features which I already acknowledge in confronting my own approaching death. In the account of Catherine of Genoa's conversion experience on March 22, 1473, her *Vita* tells us that

. . . her heart was pierced by so sudden and immense a love of God, accompanied by so penetrating a sight of her miseries and sins and of His goodness, that she was near falling to the ground . . . She saw the offended One to be supremely good and the offender quite the opposite. And hence she could not bear to see any part of herself which was not subjected to the divine justice.[6]

Not at the moment of conversion, however, but far on in the life of one whose life was a daily death into life, the great Catherine of Siena wrote of this qualitative searching in a time of prayer: "And I saw therein so much

[6] von Hügel, *Mystical Elements of Religion,* II, 105ff.

truth that my soul now confesses that I have never loved God."

The Flemish priest, Jan Ruysbroeck, adds his testimony to what these moments of prayer work in him. "To be wounded by love is the sweetest feeling and the sharpest pain which anyone can endure. To be wounded by love is to know for certain that one shall be healed."[7]

It was out of her conversion experience and its ripening life that Catherine of Genoa developed her profound doctrine of purgatory which so deeply influenced John Henry Newman and which he has immortalized in his *Dream of Gerontius*. Here Newman superbly represented this qualitative drawing and judging which the *Me* in its new awareness experiences when it has become infinitely vulnerable not alone to change and individuation but to the knife-like intensity of the love that encompasses it:

> And when—if such thy lot—thou seest thy Judge,
> The sight of Him will kindle in thy heart
> All tender, gracious, reverential thoughts.
> Thou wilt be sick with love, and yearn for Him . . .
> There is a pleading in His pensive eyes—
> Will pierce thee to the quick and trouble thee.
> And thou wilt hate and loathe thyself; for though
> Now sinless, thou wilt feel that thou hast sinned
> As never thou didst feel; and wilt desire
> To slink away, and hide thee from His sight:
> And yet wilt have a longing aye to dwell
> Within the beauty of His countenance.
> And these two pains, so counter and so keen
> The longing for Him, when thou seest Him not;
> The shame of self at thought of seeing Him—
> Will be thy veriest, sharpest purgatory.

[7] *Adornment of Spiritual Marriage*, p. 74.

John of the Cross, the sixteenth-century Spanish Car-melite whom many acknowledge as the ranking master of mystical theology, has centered upon this experience of the qualitative searching power of love, which focuses upon the *Me* in its critical moments of change, and has de-veloped his principal doctrines from it. According to John of the Cross, the pain of the application of this love to the naked *Me* is almost unbearable until the resistances to it are melted away.

One of St. John's primary objects is to expose the illusion that the nearer one approaches to God, the more pleasurable will be the effect . . . Our God is a consuming fire (Heb. 12:19) and not merely a warming and comforting one . . . When the Divine light invades the innermost spirit and pene-trates into the secret places of the heart so hidden from the soul itself, it feels its own weakness and impurity to be so great as to be set against God and God against it . . . all its once conceived goodness has vanished, its righteousness is but filthy rags . . . and it feels drawn within the flames of that bush which burns, yet is consumed not, nor consumes ought save the rubbish the soul has gathered to itself . . . it is as a piece of iron in the furnace, its impurities and rust being burnt away, for this fire of Divine love penetrates to the very substance of the soul wherein are the roots and stains of all affections and imperfect habits that it has contracted in this life.[8]

St. John believed that the dark night of the soul which that pain of qualitative searching love presses upon us here is identical with what is meant by purgatory, which a modern writer has referred to as "hell with a time limit," and that when it has seasoned the soul enough to turn

[8] Bede Frost, *St. John of the Cross,* pp. 361-363.

toward the light, and to be able to bear the light, the pain will cease "for there is nothing left to burn" and the joy of dwelling in his countenance will be complete.

There is in this no compulsion to belief in a doctrine of purgatory as an account of what comes after death. But the illumination of this intensified awareness, out of which this doctrine of a continuation of a qualitative purification arose, is one that in the face of my death as in many of the truly living moments of my life is too central to be ignored. And the doctrine itself has often appealed to many whose orthodoxy was unconnected with any institutional dogmatic system, and if it were to be called orthodoxy at all could only be described as an orthodoxy of discerning love.

LIFE IS LENT TO BE SPENT

In bringing to a close this attempt to see how death illuminates life and how life experiences are sorted out by the prospect of my own approaching death, we can scarcely leave it without noticing that many of those with a quality of life akin to these saintly ones, to whom we have just referred in order to sharpen our own perspective, have seemed to display during considerable periods of their lives an apparent fearlessness, carelessness, yes, even recklessness about whether they lived or died, or about what is to happen to them after death at the very time that they care intensely about what happens to others and are spending themselves tirelessly in the service of others.

We can, in concluding, hardly evade asking whether this disregard of death and of its consequences and this self-consuming concern for the redemption of others is, at bottom, any more than a preview of the successful at-

tainment of modern western society's attempted concealment of death and of its frantic encouragement of all to
forget their future destiny and to lose themselves here and
now in exhausting social services for the benefit of others
in the collective that we noted in the beginning. Or may it
be that these men and women, in spite of the surface
parallels, represent a response that is basically different in
kind? Much modern approval of the saints for their
vigorous championing of good causes and for their enor-
mous output of socially useful energy is quite content to
assume that their responses are not different in kind but
are the same.

Basil of Cappadocia's reply to the prefect of the Emperor,
who threatened him with confiscation of his goods, with
exile, and finally with a violent death if he would not
come over and champion the Emperor's Arian cause, is a
fair illustration of one form of this fearlessness. He sent
word to the Emperor that he would never yield, that confiscation of his goods would not affect him for he possessed little or nothing, that he would be entirely at home
with his God in any place in exile, and that as for the
Emperor's taking his life it was all but spent already and
would only hasten his communion with God. The prefect
replied that no person had ever spoken to him in this way
before. Basil answered, "Then you have never until now
met up with a Christian Bishop."

This reply of Basil of Cappadocia to the prefect scarcely
seems to have come from a man who has avoided all
thought of death or who has put his entire trust in the
social services of any collective. It seems rather to come
from a man who has for many years been a companion
of death, who has even died again and again, and who in

these deaths has had dynamically confirmed for himself the presence of a Power which is able and eager to sustain him.

I once knew a Jewish Quaker woman just over forty years of age who lived in Munich. She had all of her emigration papers in order and was at liberty to leave Germany and to enter the United States in 1938, but she decided to stay and to take a group of aged Jews into her apartment and to care for them as long as she could. She felt wholly at ease about her future when I left Germany at the turn of the year 1940-41. She had no doubt that if her present service was taken from her she would find another, and this has been the case. If her decision brought death in exile (which it ultimately did) it did not matter. But one who knew what went before in this life knew that she was one who, far from concealing evidences of death had died more than once, and hence one who lived as on a reprieve, having had bared in her that which holds when one yields to it.

Catherine of Siena in prayer again and again avowed her willingness to endure Hell forever for the salvation of those that seemed entrusted to her as she poured herself out night and day in intercessory prayer for their inward awakening. Charles Péguy, in both versions of his *Joan of Arc*, has Joan say: "If to save lost souls from the torment of eternal banishment from Thee, souls that despair in their banishment, I must devote my own soul to everlasting banishment, then, O God, let everlasting banishment be my lot." His *Mystery of the Charity of Joan of Arc* declares on the first page: "We must be saved together, we must come to God together. Together we must be presented before Him. Together we must all return to the Father's house."

John Woolman, who literally wore himself out tramping and riding over the whole span of the Atlantic seacoast from Virginia to Massachusetts and finally in England pleading for the release of negro slaves, had a dream late in his life in which he seemed to be a part of a gray mass of suffering humanity, and someone called out his name but he could not answer. Then a voice seemed to say, "John Woolman is dead." He had ceased to exist as a separate personality and had become so identified with suffering humanity that his responsibility for his fellow creatures, even to those in the animal world, was all that seemed to matter.

George Tyrrell's declaration that he did not want to be saved in the minority but to go on toiling in the agonies of the redemptive throes until the last sinner was through, is reminiscent of the early Church father, Origen, and of his unwillingness to have the redemptive process finish until all have yielded to the consuming fire of purification and been released to love. In the sixth chapter of the first book of his *De Principiis*, Origen says, "We think indeed that the goodness of God through his Christ may recall his creatures to one end, even his enemies being conquered and subdued."

Only a perverse or a blinded observer could attribute this fearlessness, this carelessness of themselves but devouring concern for others that mark these self-spending servants of men, to any socially induced anesthesia to the drastic character of death, or to the collective's encouragement of their devoting themselves to social services. They seem rather to be men and women who have died to death and to the fear of death as they have abandoned themselves to a power that vanquished death in the same breath that it called for an ever-present willingness to die and that in its service permitted them that greatest of all discoveries which the sixteenth-century poet, Robert Southwell, has congealed into a single line—"Not where I breathe but where I love, I live."

The service of others is not reminiscent of the Swedenborgian vision of Hell as that state where all were compelled to rush frantically from place to place lovelessly doing things for others. In this power to which they have abandoned themselves they have been drawn to care for others. Here they have known each other as of infinite worth and here they have yearned for each other in that which is eternal. In response to this tendering power they have sought to redeem others only again to discover their own powerlessness, their need to die again in order to have damped down in them that forward part which can die and to have raised up in them that which can alone heal the multiplicity of heart in another. Their way, then, has not been around death but through death to life in that which, if it lets them die, they do not wish to live.

I once knew a potato-grower in northern Michigan who was so frugal that he planted only the peelings of the potato for seed and fed the inside of the seed potatoes to his stock. In years when the moisture was abundant and the soil he used was good, he got a good stand of potatoes. But when a drought came on after planting, this farmer was lost. For when such a serious emergency comes, only the farmer who has planted the whole potato gets a crop. These sensitive ones who seem to live as though they knew they were *lent to be spent* dare face death as they have faced life, for they have planted the whole potato in soil which they have learned to trust.

Their word to the living is confirmed as I face the prospect of my own approaching death. For there in the prospect of change, of individuation, of qualitative searching, I am strengthened only by the gesture of the outflung arm of the sower. And in the face of death, remembering what death and life have taught me, I can gratefully repeat a line of Unamuno's, "Sow yourselves, sow the living part of yourselves, in the furrows of life."